Classic British Motor Cycles

Classic British Motor Cycles

Bob Currie

CHANCELLOR
PRESS

First published in 1984 by Temple Press
under the title *Classic British Motor Cycles: The Final Years*

This 1993 edition published by Chancellor Press
an imprint of Reed Consumer Books Limited
Michelin House, 81 Fulham Road, London SW3 6RB
and Auckland, Melbourne, Singapore and Toronto

Reprinted 1994

ISBN 1 85152 250 6

A CIP catalogue record for this book is available
from the British Library

Printed in Hong Kong

Frontispiece: Metropolitan police constables sitting on their
Velocette LEs, which became known as 'Noddy Bikes'.

The publishers are grateful to Chris Wright for
the colour photographs in this book, and many of
the black and white subjects, and to EMAP Publications
and S. R. Keig for other illustrations.

Contents

Introduction

To the present generation of motor cyclists accustomed to the products of Japan, the fact that Britain was once the king of the two-wheel world may seem almost unbelievable, yet it is the solemn truth. In all fairness, though, it should be explained that the two-wheel world of the 1950s – the period at which our home factories were at their peak – was nothing like so vast as it is today.

Certainly, BSA had every justification for advertising that their's was 'The most popular motor cycle in the world'. In 1954, for example, they were exporting to no fewer than 150 different countries. Fleet sales accounted for a useful proportion of the total, and there were BSA models in service with the Western Australia water board, the Venezuelan post office, the Yugoslavian police and the Swedish Army.

In terms of production, however, BSA were building around 75,000 machines a year, and impressive though this may sound it is barely a *week's* production by the standards of the major Japanese concerns. The total world market did indeed explode dramatically, but by the time it did, Britain's industry was already in a terminal stage.

Just why that should have happened has been probed before, and this is no place to rake over dead embers. Suffice it to say that there was no one root cause for the disaster but, instead, a combination of unhappy circumstances.

In this book models have been selected which represent the British factories, both large and small, at their classic best. Each reader will have his own preference, be it the majestic Vincent Black Prince twin or charismatic BSA DBD34 Gold Star, or sidecar man's favourite, the Panther sloper. Nor are they all roadgoing machines, for here are the immortal Manx Norton and 7R AJS racers, the 347 cc AJS trials mount which so often dominated the awards lists of the 1950s, and that incomparable all-rounder the Triumph Trophy.

Every machine was photographed especially for this volume, with the wholehearted co-operation of the National Motorcycle Museum, and all can be seen and studied 'in the metal' at the Museum's premises at Bickenhill, directly opposite the National Exhibition Centre complex, on the outskirts of Birmingham.

However, although we have picked out 25 models for in-depth investigation, this merely scratches the surface for at any one time the National Motorcycle Museum will have on display somewhere around 500 machines, chosen from a pool of three times that many. Every machine has been totally rebuilt to Earl's Court Show standard, in the maker's original catalogue colours. Moreover, these are not merely cosmetic restorations. Every bike is in full running order, and in many cases this necessitated the manufacture of new parts to replace worn-out components for which no off-the-shelf spares were available.

Many a tale could be told, too, of the ceaseless hunt for vital spares at autojumbles throughout the country, and at long-established small dealers' premises in towns big and small. To some degree, the Museum's corps of restorers had to possess the tenacity and perception of a body of Sherlock Holmses. Then what about the skill involved in restoration? If new spares were non-existent, workshop manuals and other vital pieces of literature were almost equally lacking and the

Motor Cycle's Midland editor in 1951 was George Wilson, who made good use of a 500 cc Royal Enfield twin in reporting that September's International Six Days Trial, held at Varese in Northern Italy

work had often to proceed from first principles.

The National Motorcycle Museum is a charitable trust which was founded by a retired Birmingham businessman, Roy Richards, who felt that the British motor cycle industry deserved a purpose-built museum in which glittering examples of the bikes he had known in his riding days could be shown off to maximum advantage.

Although motor cycle collections did already exist, a row of models crammed handlebar to handlebar in the gallery of a city museum was no way to show a newer generation the machines about which Dad was wont to rave. There was something soulless about dumping a few old and dusty motor cycles in one of the buildings of a farm museum, or in the stable block loose boxes of some Stately Home.

And so, over the years, the Museum collection of motor cycles came together – and not any old motor cycles, but the classics of many periods. Top-line restorers were recruited (many of them former employees of bygone motor cycle companies, with specialised knowledge of the machines on which they would now be working), and the completed machines were stored away under dust sheets in heated sheds dispersed over half a county, awaiting the establishment of a museum that would be truly worth of them.

It was the Museum Trust's bad luck that the start of their crusade to raise the necessary finance should coincide with the start of the recession, and a number of the firms which had initially promised monetary aid had themselves to trim their sails to the icy blast now sweeping through the industrial midlands. Some, indeed, would go under.

Through it all, the Trustees never lost hope that one day there would indeed be a National Motorcycle Museum, and set out to raise funds in a number of ways

Left: *one of the kingpins of the motor cycle trials scene of the 1950s, Gordon Jackson is shown here tackling Kinloch Rannoch hill in the 1956 Scottish Six Days Trial, which he won, on an AJS Model 16*

Right: *Mike Hailwood leads the 1970 Daytona 200 on a BSA Rocket 3. It was later sidelined by overheating.*

– a blitz of raffles, with tickets on sale at every Motor Cycle or Ideal Home exhibition to which they could take their van with up to a dozen examples of the restorers' art; a Friends of the Museum subscription scheme; and many more.

There was one heart-stopping occasion when Bingley Hall, Birmingham, caught fire while a number of National Motorcycle Museum bikes were being displayed at a Caravan and Camping Exhibition. Fortunately the flames did not reach the machines, but smoke and water damage meant external re-restoration had to be undertaken.

Now, at last, the dust covers have come off the stored machines, the National Motorcycle Museum exists in steel and concrete, and as the years pass it will become, more and more, a Mecca for those who would remember the great days of British motor cycles.

Bob Currie
Birmingham 1984

Designers

Hatch, H. J. ('Ike'): Chief Designer between the wars for the Blackburne engine factory at Great Bookham, Surrey, but co-operated also in the design and development of Blackburne-built engines for particular customers. These included the TT-winning Excelsior 'Mechanical Marvel', Excelsior Manxman, Coventry-Eagle Pullman, and Francis-Barnett Stag; Ike Hatch was involved also in the prototype flat-four Brough Superior Dream. He joined the development department of AMC after closure of Blackburne, and was mainly responsible for the 7R AJS racer.

Hele, Doug: Assistant to Bert Hopwood at the Norton works in the 1950s, he developed the Norton 'Lowboy' and 'Domiracer' racing machines and assisted in design of the Jubilee and Navigator twins. Invited by Hopwood to join Triumph at Meriden, he was in charge of the Daytona racing shop, and worked on the BSA/Triumph triples and the not-produced 350 cc ohc Bandit. Doug left the motor cycle industry to join Seagull outboard engines, but returned to develop the Wankel-engined Norton.

Hopwood, Bert: Spent a lifetime in the British motor cycle industry, after going straight from school to the Ariel factory. Bert was a detail draughtsman assisting Edward Turner in the design and development of the Ariel Square Four of the 1930s. His work for Norton included the vertical twin Dominator unit from which all subsequent large-capacity twins up to the final Commando were derived. Transferring to BSA, he redesigned the cylinder head of the 500 cc A7 twin, then evolved the highly successful A10 Golden Flash. In

later years Bert's work was largely administrative, but he did produce for BSA/Triumph a comprehensive modular scheme for singles, twins, and triples which failed to gain acceptance by the board. With Doug Hele, Bert designed the BSA Rocket 3 and Triumph Trident.

Page, Valentine: Possibly the most respected of all British motor cycle designers, Val Page's long career

embraced (for J. A. Prestwich) the overhead-camshaft Brooklands engines raced by Bert Le Vack in 1922 and 1923 and (for Ariel) the imaginative all-enclosed 249 cc Leader of the 1960s. Much of Val Page's life was spent with Ariel, but a spell with Triumph in the 1930s produced the 650 cc Triumph Model 6/1 vertical twin, and the range of singles from which Edward Turner evolved the Tiger 70, 80 and 90. Moving to BSA he designed the immortal M20 of Second World War military fame, and the pre-war Gold Star. After the war he returned to Ariel where his work included the 500 cc KH vertical twin.

Poppe, Erling: Son of one of the founders of the Coventry-based White & Poppe engine firm, Erling Poppe was in the 1920s a partner with Gilmour Packman in building the P & P motor cycle, but sold out and became a designer for Dennis Brothers in the commercial vehicle field. He was enticed back to BSA during the Second World War, and is best known for his design of the post-war S7 and S8 Sunbeam twins, built by BSA's subsidiary factory at Redditch. Another Poppe design for BSA was a scooter, the Dinghy, but this was not produced. Moving to Douglas, he assisted in sorting-out the problems of the first post-war transverse twins.

Turner, Edward: Starting as a motor cycle agent in south London in the early 1920s, Turner built a small series of 350 cc overhead-camshaft Turner Specials. Moving to the Midlands, he tried to interest various factories in his idea for a new type of four-cylinder motor cycle, and was eventually backed by Ariel. The machine became the illustrious Square Four. Turner refined the Val Page Ariel sports singles to produce the Red Hunter series, and was then put in charge of

Triumph by Ariel managing director Jack Sangster, after the Coventry firm had been acquired by Sangster in 1936. Turner's best-remembered work for Triumph is the 498 cc Speed Twin, a design which changed the face of motor cycling, but other designs included the Tiger Cub and its derivatives, and the Sunbeam/Tigress scooter.

Walker, Phil: Did not move around the motor cycle industry as did so many of his contemporaries, but remained with AMC (makers of the AJS and Matchless) at Woolwich. Development engineer under Bert Collier, he became a designer in his own right with the post-war AJS and Matchless vertical twins which had the unusual feature of a centre main bearing. Other Phil Walker designs included the lightweight 250 and 350 cc ohv AJS and Matchless with cylindrical gearbox.

The famous 350 cc AJS 7R racer was mainly the responsibility of Ike Hatch. Like the pre-war AJS racers, it had an overhead camshaft driven by Weller-tensioned chain, but there the resemblance ended. The gold finish of the crankcase and timing case was protective treatment for the magnesium alloy of which they were made.

1958 AJS 347 cc Model 16MC Trials

From autumn, right through the depths of winter, to the coming of spring, on virtually every Sunday and in virtually every part of the British Isles there will be hundreds of motor cyclists climbing muddy banks, teetering across rocky gullies, and balancing their way through boulder-strewn watercourses, in a rather off-beat form of two-wheeled sport known as 'trials'.

Why 'trials'? Because back around the very dawn of motor cycling it was very necessary for a fledgling motor cycle manufacturer to demonstrate how well his machine could perform, in direct competition with others. To that end, 'reliability trials' were organised – long-distance runs which would take in, along the way, whatever steep main road hills could be found. The object, of course, was to prove how reliable the machine could be in such circumstances.

But as the years went by, so *all* motor cycles grew to be reliable; and as power outputs rose, so no main road hill remained an obstacle. So, more and more 'trials' took to the minor lanes and, eventually, went off the road altogether to seek out testing climbs and hazards in private woodland, or on open mountain sides. Now, it was not so much competition between one maker and his rivals, as a test of skill of the rider irrespective of what machine he may be riding.

'Trials', more or less as we know them now, came into particular prominence in the years immediately following the Second World War, for this was a sport in which the average clubman could indulge, without the need for excessive expenditure or equipment. Often, the machine he rode would be the one he used for home-to-work travel during the week, preparation being largely a matter of removing the headlamp to prevent damage.

Gradually, however, the 'trials machine' began to emerge as a special, catalogued model. Certainly there were catalogued trials bikes in pre-war times – Levis, Baughan, and Panther among them – but they were in the minority, and not until the late 1940s did the true trials bike emerge. It was a classic overhead-valve single based on a roadster but with a woofly, flexible engine with plenty of bottom-end power.

Typical was the 347 cc AJS longstroke (69 × 93 mm), with a compression ratio lowered to 6.5 to 1 by the simple expedient of inserting a compression plate under the cylinder barrel (remove the plate, and the same machine could be used for scrambling). Initially it was unsprung at the rear, because diehard trials riders felt that with a rigid-frame machine every beat of the engine had a direct impact on the ground.

From the days when a trials machine, as catalogued, differed little from its roadster counterpart: the 1958 347 cc AJS.

Trials bikes have changed so drastically in recent times, it is hard to believe that the 347 cc AJS was one of the most successful 'bog-wheels' of its day. Note the small cylindrical toolbox carried on the engine plates above the gearbox.

It was Hugh Viney, known as the 'king of plonk' because of his ability to ride his AJS up a stony bank so slowly that virtually every rev could be counted, who led the AJS works trials team in the immediate post-war years – and it was Viney who won the 1947 Scottish Six Days Trial at his first attempt (a feat unheard-of at that time) only a couple of weeks after signing for the factory. He won again in 1948, made it three-in-a-row in 1949, then scored his fourth Scottish victory in 1953.

By that time, though, Kentish farmer Gordon Jackson had come into the AJS trials squad – and in due course he, too, would win the Scottish Six Days Trial four times (in 1956, 1958, 1960 and 1961). Jackson's last win, in 1961, is still talked about in Scottish circles, for Gordon went through the entire week for the loss of just one mark – for a single dab on Grey Mare's Ridge, a long and winding hill rising above Loch Leven.

Unlike AJS roadster models (which had hearth-brazed, lug-built frames), the trials model used an all-welded tubular frame with duplex engine cradle and rear frame loops – mainly to reduce all-up weight, but also so that protruding bits such as exhaust and footrests could be tucked-in more closely. Rear springing was added from 1955, initially with the slim type of AMC's own damper units, later with the familiar 'jampots', and then from 1957 with Girling units fitted with special yokes to marry with the AMC frame (AMC, because there was an equivalent trials model in the Matchless range, the G3LC, differing only in the tank transfers and lining colours).

That year, 1957, the 347 cc Trials had undergone quite a facelift, with a new frame which raised ground clearance from the former 7 in to a hefty 10 in; it was, too, narrower and so the exhaust could lie more closely against the lower run of the engine cradle – and that meant that the former kick-start crank, which had an exaggerated outward bend to clear the pipe, could now be discarded.

For 1958 there was no essential change, and so the machine we see here is the Model 16MC at the height of

The tiny Dunlop rubber saddle does not promise much comfort – but trials riders spent most of their time standing on the footrests, anyway. High ground clearance was necessary, to avoid rocks.

Specification

Make AJS *Model* 16MC Trials

Capacity 347 cc
Power output 18 bhp at
  5,750 rpm
Wheelbase 54 in
Tyre size: front 2.75 × 21 in; *rear* 4.00 × 19 in

Bore and stroke 69 × 93 mm
Weight (dry) 319 lb
Price when new £243 5s 3d

Suspension: front Telescopic, oil-damped
        rear Swinging-arm, with spring-and-hydraulic dampers

Manufacturer Associated Motor Cycles Ltd, 44 Plumstead Road, London SE18

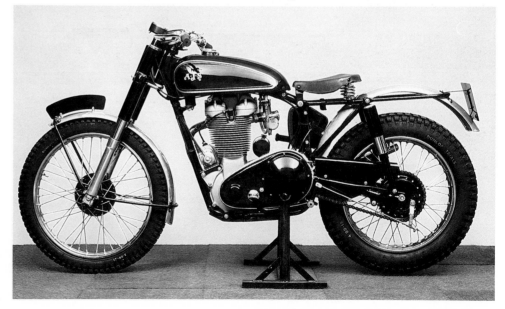

its trials fame. The previous autumn, Gordon Jackson had taken his mount to victory in the British Experts Trial, and he began the new season with a win in the snowy and muddy Victory Trial, held in Shropshire, by three marks from BSA team leader Jeff Smith. The works AJS trio were now at their most formidable, for backing Jackson there were old-stager Bob Manns, and new boy Gordon McLaughlan. Jackson and Manns both featured strongly in something new – the first-ever BBC Television Trial – but soon it was Scottish Six Days Trial time again.

At the end of the first day's run only two competitors still retained unsullied sheets, and they were Gordon Jackson on the Model 16MC AJS – and Sammy Miller on his incredible 497 cc Ariel, GOV 132. For the spectators thronging the Lochaber hillsides, the other two hundred entries were of minor interest, for all the week the real battle would involve those two men only.

Not until the Wednesday did Jackson at last shake

off his shadow and begin to draw clear – but only marginally, at that, and the event was to end with Jacko scoring his second win, and Miller in runner-up spot, only seven marks behind. From this point on, the 347 cc AJS Trials was to remain virtually unaltered, retaining its small rubber-topped single saddle to the very end of production.

The small fuel tank (carried on pillars from the standard roadster frame lugs) was just sizeable enough for a trial. An ambitious owner would have stripped off the front fork upper shrouds in the interests of weight-saving.

Evident here is the infamous sealing band of the AJS front chaincase, which rarely stopped oil leaks. The magneto is a ventilated 'wader' pattern, with breather tube carried up the front down tube of the frame to high level.

1962 AJS 348 cc Model 7R

Although there had been a road-racing Model 7R (and before that a Model R7) in the AJS programme in pre-war days, the earlier machines had little in common with the sleek black-and-gold beauty announced for the 1948 season. The exception was the common use of a chain-driven overhead camshaft, the chain tensioned by a Weller spring blade.

If anything, the new 7R gave more than a passing nod to the rival Mk. VIII racer from Velocette, which shared the same bore and stroke dimensions of 74 × 81 mm, but it was certainly lighter than the Velocette. This was due, in main, to the use of magnesium-alloy (Elektron) crankcases, timing-gear casing, and conical wheel hubs, and to aluminium fuel and oil tanks, all of which helped to bring the dry weight of the model down to a shade under 300 lb.

News of the machine broke in the weekly press in the early part of 1948, and the Plumstead factory tooled up for production very rapidly indeed. Oddly enough, it was at a *grass-track* meeting that the public had the first chance to see a Model 7R in action. The venue was Brands Hatch (at that time yet to receive a tarmac roadway) and AJS works rider and sales director Jock West put in a couple of laps of the bumpy circuit, tackling the top straight hands-off to demonstrate the machine's stability. The prototype, it was said, had already covered several hundred miles on the road.

Nevertheless, the model was essentially a road racer and very soon its performance in that field was demonstrated in the Pau Grand Prix, in the south of France, where Fergus Anderson held second until his clutch burned out. It was, of course, to be raced by the official factory team of West, Ted Frend and Les

Graham, but the 7R was primarily intended as an over-the-counter racer for the ordinary club lad. By the time the 1948 TT Week came around, production was well and truly into its stride – so much so that there were 25 AJS-mounted starters in the Junior TT, of which 18 would receive the chequered flag at the finish.

True, the official works trio failed to shine (Les Graham, in seventh place, was the best-placed of them) but private owner Maurice Cann was fifth. And there was even more elation among the 7R men when, in the Senior TT, Geoff Murdoch brought his brand-new 7R home fourth – the best performance by a 350 cc rider in that race since Howard Davies had won the Senior on a Junior mount, back in 1921.

In fact, as the years rolled by, it seemed that the 7R never would gain the greater Grand Prix glory – yet perhaps that did not matter very much, after all. Down on power it may have been, but it was a thoroughly trustworthy tool in the hands of the lesser riders,

Nicknamed the 'Boy's Racer', the handsome 348 cc AJS Model 7R is seen virtually at the end of production in 1962 guise.

In the later stages of 7R development the original oval-section frame tubing had given way to conventional round tubing. An interesting detail is the twin-feed oiler to the primary chain.

allowing the clubman a full season's sport at a minimum of maintainance cost and giving him the chance of a fair return in prize money.

In its original 1948 version the 7R was distinguishable by the enormous size of its megaphone exhaust, and by the gold-anodised finish of the main engine castings (adopted for preservative reasons, rather than for appearance). At that time the only fuel available was the dreaded 73-octane 'Pool' petrol and, accordingly, the engine had to be soft-tuned. Compression ratio was a modest 8.4 to 1, and power output an equally modest 30 bhp at 7,000 rpm.

Unusually, the duplex frame was constructed in oval-section tubing. The front fork was a development of the AMC Teledraulic fork first devised for the wartime G3L Matchless, and the swinging-arm rear suspension was controlled by slim damper units manufactured by AJS themselves (for proprietary damper units had yet to come on to the market).

The makers were well aware that the first model had considerable room for improvement, and a development programme under the control of Matt Wright was put in hand ready for the 1949 season. For one thing, there had been complaints that the rear damping

tended to grow tired. The 1949 models, therefore, adopted fatter damper units – soon to become known far and wide as 'Jampots'. Compression ratio was raised to 8.85 to 1, and the flywheel assembly revamped by using smaller-diameter flywheels (for greater acceleration and less oil-drag) and a stiffer big-end assembly. Valve angles were reduced to 74 degrees, and a smaller-diameter megaphone adopted to give greater flexibility at low revs.

For the 1949 Junior TT, the number of 7R starters had increased to 41, of which 32 finished, but that demonstration of bulk reliability was more than outweighed, publicity-wise, by the failure of Bill Doran's works mount while leading the race and only 12.5 miles from victory. Indeed, not until 1950 could AJS claim a semi-major victory, with Les Graham taking the laurels in that year's Swiss Grand Prix.

For the 1953 season a complete redesign was undertaken, resulting in a very much altered appearance. There was a new and narrower frame, with a 5.5-gallon fuel tank secured by a spring-loaded strap, and though the engine looked much as before, there were near-square bore and stroke dimensions. Moreover, Ike Hatch had devised for the works team a

The conical front hub houses a single-leading-shoe brake, the backplate of which features light-alloy scoops to direct cooling air in and out.

Specification

Make AJS *Model* 7R

Capacity 348 cc	*Bore and stroke* 74 × 81 mm
Power output 31 bhp at	*Weight (dry)* 298 lb
7,000 rpm	*Price when new* £323 17s 0d
Wheelbase 55.5 in	

Tyre size: front 3.00 × 21 in; *rear* 3.25 × 20 in

Suspension: front Telescopic, oil-damped
rear Swinging-arm, with spring-and-hydraulic dampers

Manufacturer Associated Motor Cycles Ltd, 44 Plumstead Road, London SE18

Frame redesign and (especially) a higher and longer fuel tank, lent a completely different appearance to the later 7R racers.

totally new engine with two inlet and one exhaust valves, operated by a triple-knocker arrangement.

With the three-valve, Plumstead at last claimed Junior TT success, with Rod Coleman the winner, backed by Derek Farrant on a similar model in second place. However, the machine was not really a practical proposition for production, and before shelving further development an example was taken to Montlhèry Autodrome, near Paris, where Rod Coleman, Pierre Monneret and Bill Doran established no fewer than 21 world records, including taking the 350 cc one-hour record at 115.66 mph.

From 1954 onward, former Raleigh and Vincent-HRD development engineer Jack Williams took charge of the two-valve 7R, and though working on a shoestring budget, he succeeded in pushing the power up until it was producing more than the three-valve had done. By this time, Associated Motor Cycles (the AJS parent company) was running into financial difficulties, and from 1956 it was decided that they could no longer afford to support an official racing

team. Development of the production 7R would continue, but at a lower level than before.

That was a pity, because in the years ahead the 7R would come nearer to TT success than ever before. In 1959, for instance, Bob McIntyre managed to get his 7R between the works MV Agustas of John Surtees and Mike Hailwood in the Junior TT, holding that position for four laps until vibration fractured his fairing brackets. A year later Bob Mac finished third at 95.11 mph, the fastest speed yet recorded with a 350 cc single.

Even better things were to come in 1961, this time with Mike Hailwood trying his level best to record a 100 mph lap in the Junior TT, and taking his 7R round at 96.77 mph before the gudgeon-pin broke. But, regrettably the days of the 7R were already numbered. Accountants investigating the affairs of AMC came to the conclusion that production of the 7R was a prestige exercise that could no longer be afforded, since each machine was being built and sold at a loss. So although the order book was still comfortably full, the gallant 7R was killed off.

Right: gone are the Jampot rear suspension units; now there are Girling dampers, but with specially made lower fork ends to suit Plumstead's frame. The rear brake has ventilated openings, without air scoops.

Far right: Leicester stalwart Maurice Cann could always be relied upon to finish in a leader-board place. This is 1948, first year of the AJS 7R, and he was to finish fifth in the Junior TT (going on to win the same week's Lightweight TT on a Moto Guzzi). Cann's Isle of Man career spanned the years 1938 to 1953.

1949 Ariel 997 cc Square Four

In the present-day motor cycle world, a machine with a four-cylinder (or even, as in the case of the Benelli a six-cylinder) engine placed across the frame is quite accepted practice – but that was not always so. Back in the veteran and vintage years it was reckoned that if a four-in-line engine was placed in a frame lengthwise, the resulting machine would be rather unwieldy – and besides, No. 3 cylinder, if it was an air-cooled four, tended to overheat. Alternatively, a bike with a cross-wise straight-four engine would be too wide.

But in the late 1920s a London motor cycle dealer named Edward Turner (who was also manufacturing, in very small numbers, a 350 cc overhead-camshaft single under his own name) thought of a much more compact way of constructing a four-cylinder engine. Why not, thought he, place the cylinders two by two? In effect, it would be a couple of vertical twins geared together, neither too long nor too wide.

With the 'Great Idea' sketched roughly on the back of a cigarette packet, Turner made a trip to the Midlands and tried to get first one, then another factory interested in the scheme. BSA nearly bought it, but had second thoughts. However, it was at the Ariel factory at Selly Oak that Edward Turner at last found a sympathetic ear – that of Jack Sangster, the firm's managing director.

Sangster agreed to back Turner, by providing him with a small drawing office in which to work out the design properly, together with the services of an assistant draughtsman who, in the course of time, would become a famous designer in his own right, Bert Hopwood.

The first Square Four to appear was a light 500 cc overhead-camshaft job; so light, indeed, that initial testing was done with the prototype engine housed in the frame of one of Ariel's standard 250 cc models, but for convenience when actual production began for the 1931 season the frame employed was the twin-front-down-tube design that had been evolved for a 500 cc sloper single. The engine comprised two crankshafts geared together at the middle pinions. Only the left-hand rear cylinder employed a full crank (from which, of course, the primary drive was taken), and the other three cranks were all one-sided. Cylinder block and head were iron castings, and drive to the overhead camshaft gear was by chain.

In practice, the first 500 cc model proved a little underpowered, and it was soon supplemented by a 600 cc version. Smooth and sedate the Square Four may have been, but unfortunately it did not take kindly to

Possibly the most majestic of all the Square Fours, the 1949 model retained the bright-red-panelled and chromium-plated fuel tank of pre-war days, with the post-war refinements of a telescopic front fork and all-alloy engine.

This shows clearly how the primary drive is taken from the rearmost of the two geared-together crankshafts. The chromium-plated cover on the primary drive case encloses a clutch which runs 'dry' in a compartment separate from the chaincase.

tuning for speed – mainly because the flow of air between the top of the cylinder head and the underside of the cambox was too restricted, resulting in overheating and warping.

This came to light particularly when Ben Bickell, at Brooklands, made a determined attempt to put 100 miles into an hour, thereby to claim a cup put up by *The Motor Cycle*, for the first multi-cylinder British machine to do so on British soil. There was no doubt that Bicknell's supercharged 500 cc Square Four could have won the cup – if only it could be kept running long enough. But, time after time, the cylinder head would warp, a gasket would blow, and Bickell would be sidelined again.

Similar problems befell Somerville Sikes, who entered another blown 500 cc Ariel Square Four for the 1931 Senior TT. On the bench, Sikes's engine produced 40 bhp; but in the race, he was a retirement – inevitably, with a blowing cylinder-head gasket.

Driven a little more gently, however, the Square Four could provide a superb ride, and as part of the Ariel company's 1932 Maude's Trophy demonstration, a 500 cc Square Four covered 700 miles in just under 700 minutes. Nevertheless, the manufacturers thought

Pre-war Ariel features which continued into post-war practice included the shaped front registration plate, well-valanced front mudguard, and chrome-plated fuel tank with tank-top instrument panel.

it prudent to revise the design entirely, and it was a totally different Square Four which graced the 1937 programme. Gone was the overhead camshaft, while the bottom-end assembly now featured two full-crank shafts coupled together by gears at the left-hand side, outside the crankcase proper. The new pushrod ohv machine was still available in 600 cc capacity but, the better to haul a large sidecar, it was now backed by a 997 cc version.

At this stage, and right to the outbreak of the Second World War, front suspension was by a conventional girder fork with central spring, but for 1939 a neat spring heel became available at extra cost. Devised by Frank Anstey (who had joined Ariels from the Rudge works in Coventry), it embodied coil load and rebound springs housed in the usual boxes attached to the rear sub-frame, but by an arrangement of compensating links the rear wheel spindle as it rose and fell moved in an arc, so keeping rear chain tension constant.

The Ariel sprung heel worked very well indeed, and in fact it was to remain right to the very end of Square Four production in 1958. Just two experimental models were built, using conventional swinging-arm rear suspension and damper units, but these (one of which

Specification

Make Ariel *Model* 4G Square Four Mk 1

Capacity 997 cc
Power output 34.5 bhp at
   5,400 rpm
Wheelbase 56 in
Tyre size: front 3.25 × 19 in; *rear* 4.00 × 18 in

Bore and stroke 65 × 75 mm
Weight (dry) 434 lb
Price when new £246 7s 8d

Suspension: front Telescopic, oil-damped
            rear Compensated plunger and link, undamped

Manufacturer Ariel Motors Ltd, Grange Road, Selly Oak, Birmingham 29

survives in a private collection) never reached the assembly line.

Wartime saw Ariels busy with a 350 cc single (the W/NG) for Army service and, not surprisingly, this was continued into peacetime production with the addition of a telescopic front fork. Within a very short space of time the Square Four had returned. That, too, adopted a telescopic fork and in the interests of streamlining production only the 1,000 cc model was marketed, the 600 cc version being retired.

Demand for the Square Four was steady, if not exactly world-shattering, for in one sense it was a machine that appealed particularly to the middle-aged man who, having had a motor cycle in his youth, wanted to return to the fold with something that would distinguish him from the crowd. In other words, it was very largely a status symbol rather than a model for everyday, go-to-work riding.

It must be said, too, that with the passage of time it had collected a deal of unwanted weight, so now the Selly Oak drawing office put the model through an intensive slimming course, during which no fewer than 33 lb would be shed. Mainly, of course, this was achieved by scrapping the old cast-iron cylinder block and head and substituting light-alloy castings.

This, then, is the post-war 997 cc Square Four as we see it in 1949 form, but it was not the ultimate development of the model for 1954 would bring yet another revamp, from which would emerge the Mk. II 'Four Pipe' – still with light-alloy head and barrel castings, but with an unusually attractive arrangement of two separate pipes at each side, emanating from beautifully-finned manifold castings.

As was noted earlier, the last 'official' Square Fours left Selly Oak in 1958, but that was not quite the final curtain. Two enthusiastic brothers, Tim and George Healey, established a small factory at Redditch to manufacture hard-to-find spares, and their activity culminated in production of a handful of complete Healey Fours, powered by renovated Ariel engines incorporating new parts where necessary, housed in an Egli-type frame with modern front and rear suspension.

Right: Frank Anstey designed the unique rear-springing system, in which links ensure that as the wheel spindle rises and falls, so also it moves in an arc, chain tension thereby remaining constant.

Far right: by this time the 997 cc Square Four engine had almost reached the end of its development, with the all-alloy two-pipe cylinder head and barrel (still to come was the ultimate 'four-piper'). The carburettor is a Solex, the gearbox a Burman.

1964 Ariel 249 cc Leader

Nobody meeting Valentine Page for the first time would have imagined he had anything to do with the motor cycle industry. Courtly and soft-spoken, he might have been an English school housemaster of the 'Mr Chips' variety – but in fact he was one of the most brilliant motor cycle designers that Britain has ever produced.

Val Page's successes went right back to the overhead-camshaft JAP racers of the 1922 Brooklands period, and he had first come to the Ariel works to produce, for 1926, a totally new and up-to-date range which was to take the company into the forefront of the late-vintage motor cycling scene. Later, for Triumph, he evolved a group of smart singles which Edward Turner, with cosmetic treatment, would present as the Tiger 70, 80 and 90; moving to BSA, Val designed the never-to-be-forgotten M20 side-valve, mainstay of the British Army in the Second World War, and the basic ohv single which would eventually develop into the Gold Star.

The post-war years found Val Page back at Ariel, where his first new model was the ohv vertical twin Model KH, but as the 1950s were coming to a close, so the BSA Group (of which Ariel Motors was by this time a subsidiary) decreed that Ariel four-stroke manufacture would end. For some time, though, Val Page and his drawing office staff had been at work on something totally new – a 249 cc two-stroke twin, suspended from a pressed-steel backbone frame of revolutionary concept. Laying out the works for production of the new model meant sweeping away all the older-established machines – even the revered Square Four had to go. It was, too, a necessarily expensive business, for the cost of press tools mighty enough for the quantity production of such items as the frame beam and front fork members would have daunted anyone with less drive than Ken Whistance, the one-time TT rider who was director and general manager of the Selly Oak factory.

The new machine, announced in midsummer of 1958, was of course the Leader, and the company's publicity of the time said it all: 'Designed with today's motor cyclists in mind, the Leader gives you *all* the advantages of scooter cleanliness and weather protection, coupled with *all* the performance and roadholding of the modern motor cycle.'

In one sense, the Leader was aimed at the same goal

The all-enclosed 249 cc Ariel Leader was a complete departure not only for the long-established Ariel company, but for the British industry as a whole.

Frontal aspect of the Ariel Leader is the most impressive. Shown to good effect in this view are the integral legshields and windscreen, and the pressings housing the trailing-link front fork.

as had been the Velocette Model LE – the untapped field of those who needed personal transport, but who regarded motor cycles of traditional design as 'dirty, smelly things' necessitating the rider dressing himself up in protective clothing before facing the climate.

The Leader offered such a rider a machine wherein all the working parts were totally hidden from view. Legshields and handlebar windscreen were integral parts of the bike, behind which the rider was snug and dry. And from a lengthy list of extras he could choose such luxuries as specially designed pannier luggage equipment and luggage rack, flashing indicators (which, at this time, had not been seen before on a motor cycle), a parking light, and even a six-day clock built into the pressed-steel dashboard at the base of the windscreen.

The main pressed-steel frame beam was immensely strong and comprised two half pressings in 20-gauge steel, welded along the centre line and incorporating, at the forward end, the steering head. Within the hollow beam, and reached by way of a side-hinged dual seat, was the fuel tank – a simple, unstressed pressing. An attractive, unstressed outer pressing covered the frame beam and embodied a dummy tank with a lid in

At the base of the windscreen is a parking light (white front, red rear), one of a host of optional extras available for the Leader. On the right of the dash panel is another 'optional extra', a Smith's eight-day clock.

the top face, which gave access to parcel space. Detachable panels at each side hid the engine and gearbox. Front suspension was by a trailing link fork of great ingenuity, the damper units for this being enclosed within the pressed-steel fork legs. Only the rear swinging-arm was of tubular construction.

Ariel had dabbled in the two-stroke field only briefly before (the 250 cc Arielette, killed off by the First World War), so the power unit of the Leader was something of a surprise. An inclined twin of 54 × 54 mm bore and stroke, it employed separate cast-iron cylinders with angled finning, while the crankcase/gearbox assembly was formed of precision die castings. Because a twin two-stroke requires individual crankcase compartments, the crankshaft was a two-part assembly, held together by a longitudinal Allen screw. Power output, on a compression ratio of 8.25 to 1, was 16 bhp at 6,400 rpm – quite ample for a gentlemanly tourer of this nature.

For a while the Leader sold very well indeed, and more and more little fancies were added to the catalogued list of options – a neat, chromium-plated rear bumper bar, polythene inner bags for the pannier boxes, special flat-rubber straps to secure packages to the cast-light-alloy rear carrier. The leading-link front

The Leader power unit was true unit-construction, the die-cast engine-gear assembly being suspended from a massive pressed-steel frame beam. Note the angled finning of the cast-iron cylinders.

Specification

Make Ariel *Model* Leader

Capacity 249 cc	*Bore and stroke* 54 × 54 mm
Power output 17.5 bhp at 6,400 rpm	*Weight (dry)* 330 lb
	Price when new £225 0s 0d
Wheelbase 51 in	

Tyre size: front 3.25 × 16 in; *rear* 3.25 × 16 in

Suspension: front Trailing-link, oil-damped
rear Swinging-arm, with spring-and-hydraulic dampers

Manufacturer Ariel Motors Ltd, Grange Road, Selly Oak, Birmingham 29

fork may have looked a trifle clumsy, but in fact it endowed the Leader with handling qualities of an exceptionally high order. The twin two-stroke engine was both tireless and smooth running, permitting a cruising speed of 60 mph to be maintained all day without effort (top speed, as recorded in a test by *The Motor Cycle*, was 69 mph, and it could cover the standing quarter-mile in the most respectable time of 22 sec).

In fact, only the brakes were a little below par. They were 6-in diameter front and rear, and employed the familiar Ariel system whereby an external adjuster could expand the shoes at the pivot point to take up wear; but it has to be said that the average Leader brakes tended to lack bite. All-up weight, by the way, was 300 lb.

Not surprisingly, the Leader was acclaimed the winner of the Motor Cycle of the Year Trophy for 1959, in a poll conducted by the weekly journal *Motor Cycle News*. In truth, however, the level of sales was giving the Ariel executive cause for worry. For one thing, the

Further optional extras included the chrome-plated rear bumper bar, and Lucas direction indicator lamps. Other touches included polythene inner liners for the pressed-steel rear pannier boxes.

Leader had failed to find favour in the lucrative American market, and sales to Britain alone were not really enough to pay back the huge investment in press tools that had been necessary.

So Selly Oak came up with an ingenious solution. Bernard Knight, in charge of the drawing office now that Val Page had retired, stripped the outer panelling from the Leader's massive frame beam, substituted a briefer top cover, and dispensed with the legshields, windscreen, and side panels. The result was the Arrow – a lighter and sportier version which was to take the Ariel twin through several more seasons. But the Leader itself had lost its initial market, and 1965 was to see it withdrawn from production.

The example pictured here is from the 1964 season, and represents the Leader at the pinnacle of its development, equipped with many of the de luxe items from the long list of extras available. It was, perhaps, the most superbly-presented touring motor cycle of all time.

1960 BSA 499 cc DBD34 Gold Star

One might well describe BSA's illustrious Gold Star as the bike that was just that little bit too good at its job for its own health. In clubman-racing trim as illustrated, its stamping ground was the Isle of Man Clubman's TT series – races introduced soon after the end of the Second World War, and intended to give the average club rider, mounted on the average sports-roadster motor cycle, a bit of competitive fun.

All this was fine – except that the BSA Gold Star so came to dominate the Clubman's events (in both 350 and 500 cc classes) that no other make could get a look-in. By way of illustration, there were 37 starters in the 1955 350 cc Clubman's TT: 33 of those were on Gold Stars! In the end, the situation was that if you hadn't a Goldie, you weren't serious. Since the original object of the exercise had long been lost, the organisers simply scrapped the Clubman's TT series, and that was that.

First, though, a word about the origin of the breed. In the between-wars years, it was the habit of the British Motor Cycle Racing Club to run a number of Wednesday-afternoon races at Brooklands – often with almost-nil spectator attendance, for these were simply 'races for the boys'.

However, one Wednesday in June, 1937, the programme contained a big surprise, for tucked among the entries was one 'W. L. Handley (497 BSA)'. Surprise indeed, for the great Wal Handley had retired from big-time racing a couple of seasons before; and as for BSA, they had turned their backs on racing after the debacle of the 1921 Senior TT in which all six works entries retired. Yet here was Wal, on an iron-barrel BSA Empire Star tuned to run on alcohol, and attended by members of the BSA experimental department.

Now, it was also the habit of BMCRC to award, to a rider lapping the infernally bumpy concrete Brook-lands bowl at over 100 mph in one of the races promoted by the club, a small lapel badge in the design of a gold star surrounding the magic figure '100'. Recipients of the badge were relatively few, for a ton-lap of Brooklands was a heroic achievement. Needless to say, that particular Wednesday the name of Wal Handley (BSA) was added to the list of heroes, and within a few weeks all became clear. BSA, it appeared, were developing a new 496 cc super-sports single for the 1938 season, the Val Page-designed M24 with all-alloy engine and the pushrods operating in a tapered tunnel

28

cast into the side of the head and barrel. And in recognition of Handley's ride, the new sportster became the M24 Gold Star.

The new Goldie had but two seasons in which to establish itself before the coming of war, and when peacetime returned the name was at first absent from the BSA programme. Basic overhead-valve singles were the 348 cc B31, and 499 cc B33, but soon competition versions listed as the B32 and B34 respectively, entered the range.

Then at last, in 1948, the Gold Star returned – not, at

Specification

Make BSA *Model* DBD34 Gold Star

Capacity 499 cc
Power output 40 bhp at
    7,000 rpm
Wheelbase 54 in
Tyre size: front 3.00 × 21 in; *rear* 3.25 × 19 in

Bore and stroke 85 × 88 mm
Weight (dry) 308 lb
Price when new £312 14s 5d

Suspension: front Telescopic, oil-damped
            rear Swinging-arm, with spring-and-hydraulic dampers

Manufacturer BSA Motor Cycles Ltd, Armoury Road, Small Heath, Birmingham 11

first, in 500 cc form, but as a three-fifty. As in the pre-war Goldie, the barrel and head were of light alloy, and the pushrods were housed in a cast-in tower. This was the ZB type, housed in a frame with telescopic front fork and plunger-type rear suspension, and it was catalogued in trials, scrambles, and sports-roadster guise.

Power output was 23 bhp at 6,500 rpm – and that was quite enough for a Gold Star to win the new 1949 Clubman's TT at the first time of asking, at an average speed of 75.18 mph (the rider was Harold Clark). At this time there was no 'Clubman's Goldie' as such, but BSA, alive to demand, listed a number of goodies to transform the model from a fast tourer into a useful racer. These included high-compression piston, TT Amal carburettor (and special cylinder head to suit), high-lift cams, and rear-set footrests.

As a sports-roadster, the Goldie of 1949 could return 78 mph, but the Clubman's TT modifications endowed it with a top speed of 90 mph. Naturally, there were those who were demanding a larger-capacity Gold Star, and it did appear – but initially as an International Six Days Trial machine. No fewer than ten 499 cc B34 Gold Stars won gold medals in the 1949 ISDT held in mid-Wales. Production of a 499 cc sports-roadster Goldie was soon achieved, but at first it did not achieve the same racing success as its smaller sister, and in 500 cc Clubman racing it could not yet match the Norton International, or Tiger 100 Triumph. But the time would come . . .

First appearance of a Gold Star with swinging-arm rear suspension was in July, 1952, at the ACU's selection tests for the forthcoming International Six Days Trial. Later the same year, the BB-type engine was introduced, with shorter connecting rod, and the die-cast barrel and head that had come into the range a year previously. Three of the swinging-arm-type 499 cc

Above: *the float chamber of the Amal TT10 carburettor is suspended by a thin rod from a rubber diaphragm mounting in an attempt to damp out fuel agitation.*

Left: *there was nothing sophisticated about the Gold Star's instrument layout – just a Smith's chronometric speedometer on the left, a matching rev-meter on the right, and an ammeter in the top of the headlamp.*

Right: *a 'Clubman Goldie' without clip-on handlebars was almost unthinkable! Nevertheless, the standard BSA front fork top yoke still incorporated conventional handlebar clamps.*

Far right: *the typical DBD34 Clubman set-up, with sharply swept-back exhaust pipe cutting across the face of the timing cover, rev-meter take-off from the Magdyno drive pinion, reversed gear pedal, and folding kick-start pedal.*

Goldies were prepared for the British Army team, and all three earned ISDT gold medals.

As the years passed, so Gold Star development was intensified, now with Roland Pike in charge. The CB model appeared, with massively-finned head and Amal GP carburettor. Power output was now around 30 bhp for the 350 cc, and 37 bhp for the 500 cc. Now the bigger model began to dominate clubman racing almost to the same extent as the smaller version, and at last came total dominance in the Isle of Man. In the 1954 Clubman's TT events, BSA not only pulled off a double victory but, to underline the lesson, provided the first three machines home in each class.

And now the Gold Star was approaching the ultimate, and for 1955 clip-on handlebars and the swept-back exhaust became standard wear for the catalogued Clubman model. This was the DB, but it was a racer looking for somewhere to race. For 1956, the

ACU moved the Clubman's events out of TT week proper, and they were held a week later. The following year they had gone altogether, for this was the TT's 50th anniversary, and with so much else to organise (said the ACU) they had no time for the clubmen.

But it was not yet the end of Gold Star development and at last the classic 499 cc DBD34 arrived, the change in designation indicating a further cylinder head redesign. Demand for the Goldie in both 350 and 500 cc sizes remained high, but it was a machine which demanded special attention in assembly and it was becoming uneconomic to build. Gradually, the options were phased out until, for 1963, the 499 cc DBD34GS alone remained. At the end of the season that, too, had vanished.

1970 BSA 741cc Rocket 3

In essence, BSA's across-the-frame three-cylinder Rocket (and its stable companion, the Triumph Trident) can be considered as a Triumph 'Tiger 100-and-a-half' – because the dimensions and geometry are indeed just those of Triumph's illustrious twin, with one more cylinder added.

Moreover, the power unit was mainly designed so that the best possible use could be made of existing tooling and techniques, and since the initial work was carried out at Triumph's Meriden factory, the choice of the Tiger 100 as a basis was a logical one. Externally, though, there were visual differences between the Rocket 3 and Trident, because the first version of the Trident found the cylinder block sitting bolt upright in the frame, whereas that of the Rocket 3 was canted forward at a pleasing angle; also, while the Triumph version employed a frame that was obviously derived from the single-down-tube Bonneville design, the BSA featured duplex-tube frame construction.

Designer Bert Hopwood had been toying with the idea of a three-cylinder machine for some time, and when in the late 1960s the BSA Group decided to bow to demands from the United States for a more powerful machine than those currently in production, it was a good opportunity for Bert to dust off his tentative design and, together with Doug Hele, get down to detailing the unit for production.

In any case, the time scale precluded the designing of a totally new machine from scratch, for rumours were rife that the Japanese were already contemplating the introduction of a large-capacity multi-cylinder machine to the lucrative American market. Tiger 100 practice was therefore a matter of expediency, and the influence of the earlier twin can be seen in the use of camshafts fore and aft of the cylinder block, and pushrods housed in chromium-plated tubes nestling in alcoves in the cylinder finning.

It was in the triple's bottom-end assembly that the greatest departure from existing practice was made: for smooth running a crankshaft with the crank throws set at 120 degrees to each other was chosen – and the manufacture of such a crankshaft involved a crafty piece of modern technology by BSA's smithy. The shaft was first forged in steel with all three crank throws lying in the same plane; then the shaft was reheated, and twisted at each end to bring the throws to the required angle. Unlike the twins, which employed bolted-up flywheels, the crankshaft was one-piece with integral weights.

Right: *flagship of the 1970 BSA range, the Rocket 3 had but a few short months to establish itself before the threat from Japan became overwhelming.*

Below: *in translucent red finish, the Rocket 3 was a real eye-catcher. Though some enthusiasts were lukewarm about the 'ray gun' triple-outlet silencer, it became acceptable. The chrome-plated disc on the front hub is merely decorative.*

In several other ways the Rocket 3 and Triumph Trident broke new ground, for the alternator was located at the timing end of the shaft (where, for once, it did not have to suffer the oily grittiness of the primary chaincase), primary drive was by a triple-row chain, and the clutch was a spring-diaphragm type which, because of the width of the engine, had to be carried on outrigger bearings.

Because the demand had come from the USA, it was essential that initial supplies of the new triples should be reserved for that market. Production began in the late summer of 1968, and it was not until April, 1969, that the first rush could be considered over, and first supplies could be released to British enthusiasts.

The reaction was overwhelming. *The Motor Cycle* road test showed that the Rocket 3's eager engine 'provides shattering acceleration and a top whack, with the rider tucked in as much as possible, of more than two miles a minute. And all with no more than a pleasant drone from the six tail pipes.'

Actual mean maximum speed, on a two-way run through MIRA's electronic timing lights, was 122 mph, while the standing quarter-mile was covered in 13.9 sec and reaching a terminal speed of 100 mph. Shattering

Unusually, the alternator of the Rocket 3 was housed on the left within the timing case. Under the tank nose can be seen the styled end cover (with side reflector) of the oil radiator.

acceleration indeed – although it had to be paid for in terms of a fuel consumption somewhat higher than those to which British riders had been accustomed; 54 mpg at a steady 70 mph may sound reasonable today, conditioned as we are to the dire figures returned by Japanese models, but in the 1960s, with memories of fuel rationing still lingering, it was a point worth commenting upon.

In the USA, the Rocket 3 and Trident proved to be instantly successful. Even in untuned form the three-cylinder engine produced 58 bhp at 7,250 rpm, but stripped for racing and tweaked by Doug Hele's racing department it was to earn a formidable race reputation, particularly in America's great prestige event, the Daytona 200.

In 1971, for instance, Dick Mann took his Rocket 3 to a Daytona victory at a new race record speed of 104.7 mph, while a Triumph Trident finished second and another Rocket 3 rammed home the lesson by claiming

Specification

Make BSA *Model* Rocket 3

Capacity 741 cc
Power output 58 bhp at
   7,250 rpm
Wheelbase 58 in
Bore and stroke 67 × 70 mm
Weight (dry) 478 lb
Price when new £670 0s 0d

Tyre size: front 3.25 × 19 in; *rear* 4.10 × 19 in

Suspension: front Telescopic, oil-damped
            rear Swinging-arm, with spring-and-hydraulic dampers

Manufacturer BSA Motor Cycles Ltd, Armoury Road, Small Heath, Birmingham 11

third spot. In the same race Mike Hailwood, the World Road-Race Champion who was spearheading the BSA-Triumph attack, retired with mechanical trouble – but not before leading the race for much of the time.

On the home racing scene, Ray Pickrell, Bob Heath and John Cooper, all on BSA Rocket 3s, were bringing the crowds to their feet. Pickrell won the 1971 Thruxton 500-Mile marathon; John Cooper pipped Giacomo Agostini to the line to win the Mallory Park Race of the Year, then went on to win the Brands Hatch Race of the South; and Bob Heath followed home Ray Pickrell and Tony Jefferies (on Triumph Tridents) to make it a one-two-three for the BSA Group triples in

the Isle of Man Production Machine TT.

Nevertheless, the Rocket 3 arrived just a shade too late. In the USA it had but a few short months of sales success before the arrival of the threatened 750 cc four-cylinder Honda Four. On the race track, the BSA could leave the Honda for dead, but the Japanese product was nevertheless more sophisticated – and cheaper. In any case, by midsummer of 1971 BSA was in deep financial waters, and economies dictated that the competitions shop be closed. It was the start of the run-down of the BSA Group as a whole, and all too soon the BSA name was no more to be seen on a motor cycle tank.

Yet the ghost of the Rocket 3 was to live on for a few years yet, for under the guise of Norton-Villiers-Triumph, production of the three-cylinder machines was restarted at Small Heath – using the forward sloping Rocket 3 engine configuration, instead of the upright Trident. But the name on the tank was Triumph, and BSA as such was dead.

Left: *the bifurcated exhaust pipe fitted to the middle cylinder is part of the overall three-into-two exhaust system. Note also the finned base of the crankcase assembly.*

Far left: *BSA's twin-leading-shoe front brake could be found on several other models in the Small Heath range of the 1960s. It was a very effective brake, too!*

35

1962 DMW 249 cc Dolomite II

Fated to have their name forever confused with that of a certain German-built transverse flat-twin, DMW were nevertheless as thoroughly British as it was possible to be. In fact the initials originally meant 'Dawson's Motors, Wolverhampton', and they were first seen in the late 1930s on the tank sides of a series of grass-track specials built and ridden by one 'Smokey' Dawson.

Smokey was an inventive character, and very soon he had launched into the manufacture of swinging-arm conversion kits of his own design, involving a pivoted fork combined with plunger spring boxes. Advertised in the early days of the Second World War, the conversions brought plenty of work to Smokey Dawson's little one-man business, but even so he was now about to launch into something else – a telescopic fork which he registered as the Dawson Telematic.

Meanwhile, in another part of Wolverhampton, Harold Nock (who in the 1920s and early 1930s had been associated with the Diamond and HRD marques) spent the wartime years manufacturing special fabrications for the War Office, his company being known as Metal Profiles Ltd.

With the return of peace, Harold Nock and Smokey Dawson got together to establish a much-enlarged DMW company, in premises at Sedgley (a suburb of Dudley) that had originally been a tram depot. It was not a happy partnership, for Smokey wanted to go back to his pre-war trade of building specials for the grass-

An unusual and well-thought-out feature of DMW frame design was cam adjustment at the rear fork pivot. To adjust the rear chain, the entire fork arm moved rearward, and the wheel thereby never lost alignment.

track fraternity, whereas Harold wanted to break into proper motor cycle manufacture. Initially there was some thought of reviving the old Calthorpe name (that famous old firm having gone into limbo at the outbreak of war). Indeed, the first prototype to emerge from the Sedgley tram depot was a 125 cc Villiers-powered lightweight bearing the unlikely name of 'Calthorpe-DMW' on its tank sides.

However, when production began the Calthorpe idea was junked, and the machine entered the field as plain

The design of the Earles-DMW front fork is such that the damper units are in line with the upper fork tubes. The pressed-steel centre section gives immense rigidity.

DMW. Well, maybe not so plain as all that, for DMW soon established itself as one of the 'class' machines in its field. Guiding genius was engineer Mike Riley, and it was he who devised such individual touches as DMW's patented rear fork which, by a double cam arrangement at the pivot, moved rearward as a whole when rear chain adjustment was necessary; in that way the rear wheel just could not get out of alignment.

Specification

Make DMW *Model* Dolomite II

Capacity 249 cc
Power output 15 bhp at
  5,500 rpm
Wheelbase 52 in
Tyre size: front 3.25 × 18 in; *rear* 3.25 × 18 in

Bore and stroke 50 × 63.5 mm
Weight (dry) 298 lb
Price when new £202 8s 0d

Suspension: front Telescopic, undamped
           rear Swinging-arm, with spring-and-hydraulic dampers

Manufacturer DMW Motor Cycles Ltd, Valley Road, Sedgley, Dudley, West Midlands

Dudley-built, the DMW Dolomite was possibly the most handsome of all Britain's post-war lightweights.

The frame of the typical DMW was extraordinarily strong, and was a combination of square-section tubing and a pressed-steel centre structure. An unusual (and unusually comfortable) dual seat was hinged at the rear, and when raised revealed a cavernous space for toolkit or small parcels.

Meanwhile, having pioneered the telescopic fork in Britain – for lightweights, anyway – the Metal Profiles side of the DMW company's operation now went into production with a whole range of telescopic forks, a business in which they are still employed. They took up the manufacture, also, of a lightweight form of Earles pivoted front fork of remarkable gracefulness, and an example of the Earles-DMW fork (which could be fitted to any DMW model as an extra-cost option) is seen on the 249 cc Dolomite II twin in the National Motorcycle Museum collection.

At this point, perhaps an explanation of the model's name might be advisable. It so happened that in the 1950s Harold Nock had spent a holiday in the town of Cortina, high in the Dolomite Mountains of Northern Italy, and so when DMW introduced a new 225 cc de luxe roadster to the range a little while later, he named it the DMW Cortina. The next newcomer was a 249 cc twin-cylinder version of the same model, and this became the DMW Dolomite. (The DMW factory was advertising the Cortina and Dolomite long before the Ford and Triumph car companies thought of using the same two names on four-wheelers; DMW did not steal the names, it was entirely the other way about!)

The 249 cc Villiers 2T twin which powers the Dolomite was first announced in 1956. Only a couple of miles along the road from the Villiers plant, DMW were naturally the first British factory to make use of the sleek Villiers engine. Crankcase mountings were identical to those of the 225 cc Mark 1H unit of the

Cortina, and so the Dolomite was just a natural extension of the DMW range.

Delightfully smooth in action, the 2T was a most likeable engine which gave very little trouble indeed in use, well able to cruise in the lower sixties, and with 70 mph available in reasonably favourable circumstances. It was a great pity, really, that Villiers felt obliged to tinker with the design in the hope of getting a still greater power output, for the subsequent 249 cc Mark 4T twin was never as charming an engine as its predecessor. It had an extra helping of power, but at the expense of harsh delivery, and a loss of flexibility.

The DMW company felt the change of power unit deeply, for they had been building (in addition to the Dolomite II) an unusual scooter-like machine, the 2T-powered Deemster, which found favour with the Mid-Wales and Staffordshire police forces as a quiet rural patrol machine, with ample space within the bodywork for the rider to stow waders, report cards, first-aid kit,

Left: named after its originator, Ernie Earles, the pivoted-type front fork was claimed to give enhanced steering qualities.

Far left: this is the 249 cc Villiers Mk 2T two-stroke twin, with smooth rounded side covers which impart a 'power egg' aspect, though in fact the separate gearbox is bolted to the engine and is not true unit-construction.

and so on. With the change of power to the 4T, the Deemster was no longer suited to this type of work, and after an unsuccessful attempt to employ the flat-twin Velocette Viceroy unit, the machine went out of production.

With the model name now changed to the DMW Sports Twin, the 4T-powered Dolomite continued into the late 1960s, and a smart little model it was, with plenty of the little attentions to detail that had made the DMW name so admired by those who appreciated quality. But the cessation of proprietary engine manufacture by Villiers was to leave DMW in the same boat as Cotton, Dot, and other small British makers – bereft of suitable power units. So the motor cycle side of DMW closed down (except for a handful of trials models, using an engine of DMW's own make, in the 1970s); but the firm still continues in business, overhauling engines and supplying Villiers spares.

1947 Douglas 348 cc Model T35

To the enthusiast with memories of the between-wars British industry, it was a big surprise that Douglas should have returned to the market at all after the end of the Second World War. Following the heady years of the mid-1920s, the company had lurched from one financial crisis to another; the last of these had occurred in 1936 when the Bristol-based firm had been acquired by Aero Engines Ltd, a concern which was hoping to manufacture Hispano-Suiza aircraft engines under licence and, pending orders, kept just a small trickle of motor cycles in production and selling these through one outlet only, Pride & Clarke, the big South London dealers.

The aircraft-engine contract never did materialise, but nevertheless the war did improve Douglas fortunes considerably. Among their wartime products was a

portable generator unit for the War Office, powered by a 348 cc flat-twin overhead-valve engine (one such generator set was reputedly used, alongside Cairo's famous Sphinx, at one of Sir Winston Churchill's celebrated summit meetings).

When it became clear that the war years were drawing to a close, Douglas turned their thoughts to peacetime production, and use of the generator engine in a motor cycle frame was an obvious solution. The post-war Douglas, the Model T35, was announced in the press in September 1945, and the machine was unlike any previous Douglas – except, maybe, the Endeavour of 1935–36 (which was a side-valve, anyway). It maintained the marque's tradition of a flat-twin layout, but the bulk of Douglas production, though, had been of bikes with a fore-and-aft cylinder layout, whereas the newcomer had the cylinders lying transversely, in BMW style.

The designer was George Halliday, who was the patentee also (jointly with the Douglas factory) of a unique sprung frame employing torsion bars. The torsion bars were carried inside the straight lower run tubes of the duplex cradle frame, and were anchored at their fore ends. At the rear, the bars were connected by short links to the fork legs of the swinging-arm frame. As the fork (a substantial box-section fabrication) rose and fell, so the movement was controlled by the twisting imparted to the torsion bars.

Originally Halliday had intended that there should be a torsion-sprung front fork also, but construction of this was too complicated. Instead the factory settled for the so-called Radiadraulic fork, with the front-wheel spindle carried on short leading links pivoted at the

Douglas were traditionally builders of flat-twin engines but the T35 broke new ground, being the factory's first across-the-frame ohv design.

Left: the very low build of the Douglas transverse twin, thanks to the engine disposition, is clearly seen. Note, under the footrest, the slotted outlet from the 'woffle box' cast-light-alloy silencer.

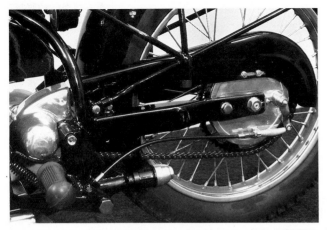

rear of the fork stanchions, and with springs and damping mechanism concealed within the stanchions themselves. Use of such a wheel mounting meant that it was difficult to arrange for the front mudguard to rise and fall with the wheel and so, instead, a fixed mudguard with deep side valances was employed.

The gearbox was built in unit with the engine and incorporated a single-plate clutch, but although it might have seemed logical to complete the job by incorporating shaft final drive – which Douglas

Specification

Make Douglas *Model* T35

Capacity 348 cc
Power output 21 bhp at
   6,000 rpm
Wheelbase 54.25 in
Tyre size: front 3.50 × 19 in; *rear* 3.50 × 19 in

Bore and stroke 60.8 × 60 mm
Weight (dry) 394 lb
Price when new £158 15s 0d

Suspension: front Leading-link, oil-damped
          rear Swinging-arm, torsion-bar sprung

Manufacturer Douglas (Sales & Service) Ltd, Hanham Road, Kingswood, Bristol

themselves had done with the short-lived Endeavour – there was, instead, a pair of bevels at the rear of the gearbox, to permit chain final drive.

One big advantage of the flat-twin engine layout is that the centre of gravity is lower than on a more conventional motor cycle, which makes for better stability on the road, and also it allows for the whole bike to be low-built. But there are also disadvantages in arranging the engine with the crankshaft in line with the frame, for at tickover speeds side-to-side shake becomes quite pronounced.

It must be said, too, that an engine designed to work at one constant speed for generating purposes, is not necessarily happy when trying to cope with varying loads and speeds as demanded by motor cycle use. For these reasons, and because workmanship was generally poor, the Douglas T35 as it reached the market was, in all honesty, not a very good motor cycle. It did have quite a good spring frame, however, and purchasers of the model could (and did!) indulge in the

Left: *the box-section pivoted rear fork appears conventional, but is coupled by short links to the rear of torsion bars carried within the frame lower-run tubes.*

Below: *on the T35, the Douglas name was cast into the rocker covers, but this disappeared when a kidney-shaped cover was employed on the reworked Mk III engine.*

novelty of riding over kerbs and bricks while boasting of the comfort to their rigid-frame-owning friends.

To their credit, Douglas (which, by the way, had just undergone yet another financial reconstruction) did do something about improving the power unit by engaging Erling Poppe, the designer of the post-war Sunbeam, as technical director. At the same time the immortal Freddie Dixon, an expert on combustion-chamber shape, was brought in as a consultant. A new cylinder head, together with flat-top pistons and a distinctive kidney-shape rocker cover which no longer bore the inset Douglas name, gave the engine a much more satisfactory performance.

This, then, was the Mark III, new for the 1949 season. The deeply-valanced front and rear mudguards were retained, as also was the flat cast-light-alloy silencer (known to Douglas enthusiasts as the 'woffle box') mounted underneath the engine. Other improvements had been made – visibly, such as a chromium-plated fuel tank, and invisibly by a general tightening of quality control.

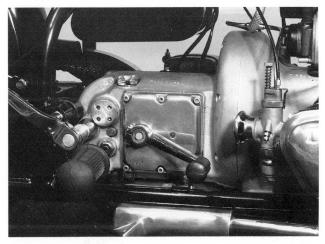

Also, there was now not just the one Douglas, but three. Partnering the roadster was the Mark III Sports, distinguished by high-level exhausts which first curved upwards then ran in a direct straight line to finish in paired tubular silencers. Although the front mudguard was still of fixed design, it had shallower valances, and both front and rear guards were finished in silver lacquer. In the opinion of many riders, the Mark III Sports was quite the nicest of the post-war Douglas breed – and it was certainly quick enough, in the hands of Don Chapman, to give the Bristol firm their only really notable clubman-racing success, at Silverstone.

Third of the 1949 Douglas range was, rather surprisingly, a trials model with a totally new frame with rigid rear end, and the motor carried high so that the cylinder heads should not clonk boulders. But though the firm tried hard, even mounting an official team in big national trials, the Trials Douglas was not really in the same league as, say, a BSA B32 or 347 cc AJS. After a couple of hopeful but unrewarding years, it was dropped.

The transverse flat-twin Douglas continued to early 1957, latterly as the totally-redesigned Dragonfly, but by then the works had changed hands yet again and the new owners had no interest in motor cycles.

1961 Francis-Barnett 249 cc Cruiser

Although a number of British factories in pre-war times were tempted to try building a motor cycle with all the working parts enclosed behind smooth pressed-steel covers – there were the New Hudsons of 1931–33, the Triumph Silent Scouts, the Excelsior Viking, the Coventry-Eagle Pullman, and several more – the public in general failed to respond, in spite of the apparent attraction of a machine which kept the rider free from oilstains and road dirt, and which could be washed down with a garden hose.

But there was just one all-enclosed model which did attract a sizeable following, sufficient to keep it in production continuously from its introduction in 1933, to the coming of war in 1939. This was the handsome 249 cc Francis-Barnett Cruiser, a Bill King design powered by a flat-top-piston Villiers single-cylinder two-stroke. Very extensive mudguarding, and curvaceous built-in legshields, helped to keep the rider dry in all weathers, while a bulbous cast-aluminium expansion box at the front, marrying with the rounded lines of the detachable engine bonnets, ensured that the Cruiser's progress was as silent as made no matter.

With the exception of the short-lived 250 cc ohv Stag (which used an engine made exclusively for Francis-Barnett by Blackburne), the models from Coventry's Lower Ford Street works had always relied on proprietary power units, so when peace came once more and Francis-Barnett could resume motor cycle production, it was 'back to the good old Villiers'. Customers who remembered and loved the 249 cc Cruiser of the 1930s pleaded for it to be brought back into the catalogue, but there was a snag. The Villiers post-war range of engines no longer included a two-

fifty, and so Francis-Barnett had to settle for the 125 cc Plover and 197 cc Falcon models.

By the 1950s both Francis-Barnett and their lightweight rivals, James, had been taken into the Associated Motor Cycles combine, although retaining autonomy for the time being. Between them, Francis-Barnett and James were by far the largest customers for Villiers motor cycle engines – a fact that seemed to annoy the parent AMC group, for they took the unprecedented step of hiring an Italian designer (Vincente Piatti) to produce a two-stroke unit that would be built in AMC's Plumstead works. Whatever they may have thought privately, Francis-Barnett and James had to toe the line, drop their Villiers-powered models, and substitute the new AMC units.

First of the Plumstead two-strokes was a 171 cc, and Francis-Barnett saw a chance to bring back the Cruiser name – in part, at least – by adding a 171 cc AMC-

With valanced front guard, maxi-skirted rear, and legshields, little enough of the Francis-Barnett Cruiser 84 could be seen by the onlooker!

Though enclosure of the rear wheel was fashionable in 1961 (even Triumph and Norton adopted it), it was carried to extremes in the Cruiser 84. Pillion footrests, when folded in the up position, disappeared into cavities in the enclosure panels to present a flush finish.

engined Light Cruiser to the range. Name apart, though, it bore no relation to the beloved pre-war job, and the 'power egg' engine unit – quite smart, really, with its smoothly rounded castings – was in no way enclosed.

Gradually the range of engines was increased, and although the 171 cc unit was dropped at the end of 1959, there was now a full house of 149, 199 and, at last, 249 cc AMC singles.

Now Francis-Barnett felt fully justified in reviving the old Cruiser name, and from 1955 the Cruiser 80 was the flagship of the roadster range, handsome in the Arden Green livery which now characterised all the Lower Ford Street products. The frame of the Cruiser 80 was a composite design, with an oval-section pressed-steel front down member and mid-section fabricated from further pressings, allied to a duplex-loop tubular rear subframe.

But as the 1950s ran to a close, so there came a move to popularise rear wheel enclosure. Triumph started it, with the 3TA Twenty-One twin, and the Triumph 'bath tub' rear enclosure was eventually to spread to virtually every model in the Meriden range except (thankfully) the Trophy and Bonneville. Even Norton joined the trend by casing-in the rear wheel of the De

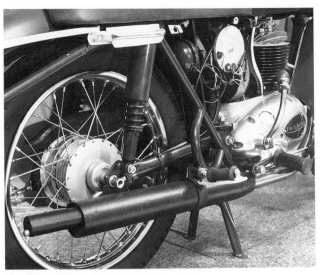

Use of outer panelling did mean that there was no necessity for the electric wiring to be tidy! Also, since the silencer would be hidden, the expense of having it chromium-plated was avoided.

Luxe Dominators (aided and abetted by Francis-Barnett, it should be said, for Norton's enclosure panels were produced for them by the Coventry concern).

Strangely enough, although Clarendon Pressings was a Francis-Barnett subsidiary, when the Fanny-B did join the enclosed-rear-wheel brigade for the 1961 season, the rear panels were not in pressed-steel, but in the new wonder material, glass-fibre. However, the 1961 Cruiser 84 did provide some work for the pressings factory, for there was a peculiarly styled front mudguard formed from a pair of seam-welded pressings. Also, the mid-section enclosure panels were arranged to come right up to the rear of the cylinder barrel and so enclose the carburettor and air cleaner (a tickler-button extension was provided, so that the carburettor could be flooded in time-honoured manner, for the first start of the day).

Lending a flush finish to the top of the fuel tank was a filler cap which, at a half-turn, raised itself by cam

Specification

Make Francis-Barnett *Model* Cruiser 84

Capacity 249 cc
Power output 12.5 bhp at 5,000 rpm
Wheelbase 51.5 in
Tyre size: front 3.25 × 18 in; *rear* 3.25 × 18 in

Bore and stroke 66 × 72.8 mm
Weight (dry) 307 lb
Price when new £180 17s 3d

Suspension: front Telescopic, undamped
           rear Swinging-arm, with spring-and-hydraulic dampers

Manufacturer Francis & Barnett Ltd, Lower Ford Street, Coventry

action. Other neat little touches included a two-stage centre stand, and a rear registration plate which, upon removal, revealed an arch through which the rear wheel could be extracted. Not that the glass-fibre side panels were difficult to remove, for each was attached by five Dzus fasteners released by a half-turn of a coin.

Another nice feature was that the dual seat was located at the front on two pegs, while at the rear was a single Dzus fastener; half a turn with a coin, yank the seat rearward and upward, and a capacious tool kit – including a tyre inflator – was disclosed. And one last point to note; when no passenger was being carried, the flat-bottomed pillion rests folded away flush with the side panelling to provide a smooth surface.

For the new Cruiser 84, a two-tone colour scheme was adopted, with the traditional Arden Green (black was an alternative) contrasting with off-white for the lower part of the tank and the lower sections of the panelling. On the road, a reasonable cruising speed of 55 to 60 mph was attainable, with a maximum speed of 65 mph. It was, maybe, a shade overgeared, but acceleration was never intended to be the Cruiser's strong point, and the high gearing did bring the advantages of fuel economy and a lazily-turning engine (88 mpg in give-and-take conditions was most commendable).

But the days of Francis-Barnett as a separate entity were already numbered. Although the Fanny-B's contribution to AMC's overall finances was a healthy one, the group as such was running into trouble, and to conserve resources the Coventry plant was closed down and Francis-Barnett, now with a much-reduced programme, was moved in with James at Greet, Birmingham in 1962. The Cruiser 84 was one of the casualties of the move, after little more than a year of production.

Above: *the flush-fitting fuel filler cap had a cam action, half a turn being enough to raise it to operational position.*

Left: *the rather angular front mudguard (used also on the Norton Jubilee) was formed from a pair of edge-welded pressings. Overall appearance is spoilt slightly by the use of too small a headlamp.*

1952 Excelsior 244 cc Talisman Sports

With good reason, Excelsior always claimed that they were Britain's oldest-established firm of motor cycle manufacturers. In fact the founders, Messrs Bayliss, Thomas, and Slaughter, had learned their trade in the country's first-ever bicycle factory (that of James Starley, in Coventry) before setting up in business for themselves in 1874 as makers of penny-farthing 'ordinary' cycles.

Before the turn of the century, they had entered the motor cycle field, from 1897 onward as producers of MMC-powered machines which soon earned quite a reputation in the very early races at cycle dromes. The trade-mark chosen was of a mountaineer standing on a peak and waving (as Longfellow wrote, in his much-quoted poem) 'a banner with a strange device, Excelsior!'

Excelsior moved from their Coventry factory immediately after the First World War – whereupon a newly-established firm called Francis & Barnett promptly moved into the vacated works in Lower Ford Street – when they were taken over by R. Walker & Sons of Tyseley, Birmingham. The Walker family had earlier built Monarch motor cycles, and for a number of years they seemed content to coast along with a modest programme of road-going models using bought-in engines by JAP, Blackburne, or Villiers.

In the 1930s, however, Excelsior cut loose and made a lunge towards road-race fame with first the 'Mechanical Marvel' and later with the famous overhead-camshaft Manxman racers, a joint design by Ike Hatch of the Blackburne company, and Eric Walker of Excelsior. To the general public the Manxman models (and the corresponding pushrod roadsters like the Warrior and Norseman) were Excelsior-built through and through. In truth, however, Excelsior had no engine-building facilities of their own and the engines were built exclusively for them, at first by Blackburne and later by Beans Industries.

The coming of the Second World War brought a

First in the field with a 250 cc two-stroke twin, Excelsior stole quite a march on Villiers, whose 2T unit was still a long way off.

Engine manufacture was entirely by Excelsior, but the bolted-on gearbox is of Albion make, and the alternator on the right-hand end of the crankshaft is by Wico-Pacy.

boost to Excelsior's fortunes, for in addition to building thousands of 98 cc autocycles (used by air-raid wardens, district nurses, munitions workers, and the like) they received a contract to make the Welbike folding scooter for the British Airborne forces. Both the autocycle and the Welbike employed the 98 cc Villiers JDL engine, but on the return of peace Excelsior at last

The styling of the Excelsior Talisman is relatively elegant, but the 'ears' at the front of the dualseat are unfortunate.

Specification

Make Excelsior *Model* Talisman Sports

Capacity 244 cc *Bore and stroke* 50 × 62 mm
Power output Not recorded *Weight (dry)* 240 lb
Wheelbase 50.5 in *Price when new* £173 15s 7d
Tyre size: front 3.00 × 19 in; *rear* 3.00 × 19 in

Suspension: front Telescopic, undamped
            rear Plunger, undamped

Manufacturer The Excelsior Motor Co Ltd, Kings Road, Tyseley, Birmingham 11

established their own engine workshops and began building the 98 cc Spryt and Goblin engines. Later came a 149 cc two-stroke single then, for the 1950 season, a 244 cc vertical-twin two-stroke known as the Talisman.

It caused a minor sensation, for except for the water-cooled Scott and the short-lived 350 cc AER of the late 1930s, no other British firm had built a two-stroke vertical-twin previously. Of 50 × 62 mm bore and stroke, the twin had a built-up crankshaft running on five main bearings, and featured three-piece crankcase construction. The cast-iron cylinders were independent, and each had its own light-alloy cylinder head. An Albion four-speed gearbox was bolted to a vertical facing at the rear of the crankcase, to give semi-unit construction. Primary drive was by duplex chain, and on the right-hand end of the engine shaft was a rather ugly Wico-Pacy flywheel alternator.

The frame was largely lug-built and hearth brazed, and featured an unusual form of rear springing in which the spring boxes (which, of course, carried the rear-wheel spindle) travelled up and down, on fixed rods clamped top and bottom. The front fork was Excelsior's own telescopic design, and was undamped.

Later in the initial 1952 season the basic Talisman TT1 was joined by a rather more sporting, twin-carburettor version, the STT1 as pictured here. More expensive than the TT1, it boasted rubber gaiters on the front fork, and a none-too-pretty dual seat instead of a single saddle. Also, in place of the traditional maroon and cream finish, the STT1 could be supplied in an attractive shade of beige with red tank lining.

The next season, 1953, saw the coming of swinging-arm rear suspension and as the years rolled by there would be a 328 cc Talisman and the factory would join the craze for rear wheel enclosure by adding midriff tinware. There would also be one or two foolish touches (such as a toolbox recessed into the tank top, with a snap-on lid which was supposed also to serve as a fuel filler cap, but which leaked dreadfully), and through it all the Talisman would maintain a modest coterie of customers. No doubt it could have been developed into a very pleasant potent little model indeed, but Excelsior never did have the money to go in for major development.

Road-tested by *The Motor Cycle*, the 244 cc STT1 Talisman Sports produced a top speed of 64 mph (with a 30 mph consumption figure of 96 mpg), and present-day riders might well turn up their noses in derision. But it has to be judged by the standards of the day, and in 1952 a 64 mph top whack was not at all to be jeered at. It was, too, a far more flexible motor than the buzz-boxes of today, so although acceleration was not exactly sizzling – 23 seconds to cover the standing quarter-mile – it was reasonably respectable.

Perhaps, had the Excelsior factory employed a stylist, the result could have been a shade more

Left: individual cylinders (cast-iron) and heads (light-alloy) are carried on a crankcase housing a built-up crankshaft with centre main bearing. Exhaust pipe clamps to the cylinder barrels seem a little over-elaborate.

Far left: the plunger-type rear springing is unique, in that the fork end and spring box travel up and down a fixed rod. Note the old style brazed-lug frame construction employed by Excelsior to the end.

aesthetic, but it was not a lack of demand that brought the end of the Talisman, but rather the financial difficulties of another company entirely – Berkeley Caravans, to which firm Excelsior had been supplying quantities of a 492 cc three-cylinder Talisman power unit (with *seven*-bearing crankshaft), for the Berkeley Sports three-wheeler. Let down by their USA importer, Berkeley went bust, owing Excelsior thousands of pounds. And there was little Excelsior could do but go bust themselves, and sell the name and the shell of the concern to Britax, the motor accessory manufacturers.

1963 Greeves 246 cc ISDT Special

Not all of Britain's once-great motor cycle industry was located in the Midlands. There was, for example, one small but enterprising part of it based at Thundersley, not far from the Essex seaside resort of Southend. In that unlikely home could be found Greeves Motor Cycles, presided over by Bert Greeves.

In reality the motor cycles were something of a sideline, for the main business of the Greeves factory was the production of three-wheeled invalid cars for the Ministry of Pensions, and bikes had to be fitted into the production schedule as best they may. Bert had been an enthusiastic motor cyclist in younger days, and he had always had an ambition to become a motor cycle manufacturer in his own right. As the Invacar business grew, so the opportunity arose for Bert Greeves' ambition to become reality, and the first highly unorthodox Greeves motor cycle prototype came into being in mid-1951, using rubber-in-torsion springing at both front and rear.

Really, the bike was an extension of the invalid car side, for the rubber springing was used also on the tricycles. But motor cycle production was still some way off, for that did not get under way until the autumn of 1953. From the start the Greeves broke new ground by featuring a unique frame in which the steering head and front-down member were combined in a massive cast-light-alloy I-section beam; the tubular frame top member was inserted into the mould, and the main frame beam was cast around it, making for a very robust construction. There was novelty, too, in the front fork, which featured short leading links to carry the wheel, pivoting on rubber-in-torsion spring units.

In fact the frame beam, in LM6 silicon-aluminium alloy, was the product of the new light-alloy foundry that had been added to the Greeves factory. It was claimed to have a strength-to-weight ratio superior to that of tubular steel, and in practice it proved to be capable of withstanding the roughest treatment that could be meted out in international competition.

Though Greeves started out by manufacturing Villiers-engined roadsters, a scrambler and a trials mount had been added by the time the new marque made its public debut at the 1954 Earls Court Show, and in the years ahead the competitions side was to dominate Greeves production more and more. Motocross was the firm's special domain, with riders like Dave Bickers, Bryan Wade and Vic Allan ensuring that the Greeves name was well to the fore; but trials were certainly not neglected. Greeves even made a successful entry into road-racing with the 250 cc Silverstone

Riding numbers displayed on the 1963 Greeves ISDT Special are those carried by British Vase B team member Triss Sharp in that year's event in Czechoslovakia.

The short front mudguard in glass-fibre is a typical product of the Greeves factory's extensive glass-fibre workshops (where Invacar three-wheeler bodies were built).

52

and 350 cc Oulton models – not fast enough to be world-beaters, perhaps, but so thoroughly reliable that they were chosen to be the standard mounts for pupils of the Mortimer Road-Racing School.

Pictured here is a machine from a different sporting field again, the world of the International Six Days Trial, rightly described as the toughest competition any machine had to contest. The year is 1963, and the little Greeves factory had been paid the great honour of being asked to provide machines for two of the men who would be representing Britain in the International Vase 'B' Team; honour indeed, for up to this point Britain had always relied on much heavier metal in the ISDT – invariably four-stroke, and usually vertical twins.

The selected riders were Triss and Brian Sharp (sons of pre-war Crystal Palace Speedway captain, Triss Sharp Snr), but the Greeves factory took the opportunity to prepare three machines for the event, which on this occasion was to be held at Spindleruv Mlyn, in the Czechoslovakian mountains. The third bike was for Peter Stirland who, with Triss and Brian, would make up an official Greeves trio competing for manufacturer-team awards.

The machine in the National Motorcycle Museum collection carries the 1963 ISDT riding number of Triss Sharp.

The basis of the Greeves ISDT model was the 246 cc Model 24MDS Scrambler, although with a number of modifications to make it more suited to its role of mechanised mountain goat. The frame was the usual Greeves design, complete with cast-light-alloy front beam; the front fork had the usual short leading links (with strengthening loop around the rear of the front wheel), pivoting in rubber-in-torsion bushes and controlled by spring/damper units housed within the

fork stanchions.

In essence the engine was the Villiers Mk 36A, but highly modified. Instead of the standard Villiers crankshaft there was an Alpha assembly with full-circle flywheels, while sitting on top of the Villiers crankcase was a very square-looking light-alloy cylinder barrel and head (products, of course, of Greeves' own foundry). The ISDT regulations call for an operative lighting set, and so the Villiers flywheel magneto incorporated lighting coils and a small headlamp was mounted behind the front competition

The rocking-pedal gear change is interesting, permitting the rider to change gear while standing on the rear mounted footrests.

number plate (which could be flipped up to allow the lamp to shine when called upon to do so).

Ingeniously, an emergency ignition system was incorporated, with a coil and condenser tucked away under the fuel tank; should the flywheel magneto fail, the emergency coil could be energised from the lighting coils. Finally, before being shipped out to Czechoslovakia the engine-gearbox assemblies of all three works models were given a coating of matt black heat-dispelling paint.

It is part of the ISDT tradition that once a machine has been weighed-in on the day before the start of the trial, it is parked in the open in an enclosure from which competitors are excluded until only minutes before they are due to start. That first night proved to be rainy, and although the day of the trial dawned bright and dry Triss Sharp was unable to start his machine within the time permitted, and had to forfeit 20 points by push-starting. Worse was to come within minutes, for poor Triss got no further than five miles from the start before he was out of the trial, with the big-end seized.

This was disaster for Britain, although Greeves honour was retrieved to some extent by Brian Sharp and Peter Stirland, who went right through the week without dropping a point, to be awarded with gold medals. A privately-entered Greeves, ridden by the sole lady entrant, Mary Driver, gained a bronze medal.

Greeves motor cycle production continued until well into the 1970s (in 1975, they built a batch of 380 cc Greeves Griffons, to be used by the Royal Artillery Motor Cycle Display Team), but the firm was struck a body blow when the Ministry of Pensions decided that invalid tricycles were out, and that in future the disabled would be issued with specially-modified four-wheeled cars. In any case, founder Bert Greeves had already retired from work, soon to be followed by his cousin (and Greeves sales director) Derry Preston-Cobb, and motor cycle making was brought to a halt in 1978.

Far left: *another Greeves hallmark – the leading-link front fork, pivoting in a rubber bush, and with slim damper units hidden within the fork stanchions.*

Left: *the cast-light-alloy front down beam incorporating the steering head was for many years a trade-mark of Greeves design. The engine has a Greeves cylinder barrel and head on a Villiers crankcase assembly.*

1955 Matchless 498 cc Model G45

In one respect the ambitious amateur road-racer of the immediate post-war period was, if he preferred Norton machinery, laughing. Norton could offer him the famous Manx in both 350 and 500 cc capacities, so with a machine of each size on his trailer he could go to a meeting with the anticipation of having a full day's sport. But he who supported the products of Associated Motor Cycles was at a disadvantage. There was the admirable AJS Model 7R for the 350 cc races, but having said that . . .

With hindsight, one might well ask why Plumstead did not just enlarge the very satisfactory 7R and produce an equally satisfactory 500 cc version. Indeed, they were to do that very thing in 1959, the G50 overhead-camshaft racing single being simply a 7R (same bottom end, same stroke, but with a bored-out barrel) with a red instead of black fuel tank.

But that was later. Top dog in the 1951 touring catalogue was the 498 cc Model G9 Super Clubman vertical-twin ('The twin that has set a new standard in performance, road-holding and comfort', if one could believe the Matchless advertising of the time) and it could well have been that the factory gaffers felt that a successful racing vertical twin could reflect favourably in sales of the production tourer.

On the other hand, it may have been just the inbuilt Matchless instinct to do things on the thinnest of shoestring budgets. Whatever, the summer of 1951 saw Ike Hatch and the Plumstead experimental shop engaged on development of a racing version of the Phil Walker-designed G9. Perhaps it should be explained here that the Matchless differed from all other vertical-twins in featuring a three-bearing crankshaft – roller

outer bearings, plus a plain centre bearing carried in a web between the two crankcase halves. The cast-iron crankshaft had two integral flywheels (one either side of the main bearing) plus bobweights at each side. The cast-iron cylinders, and light-alloy cylinder heads, were separate, not cast in monobloc.

The immediate aim of the experimental department was to produce a one-off G9 racer with which Robin Sherry could contest the 1951 Senior Manx Grand Prix, but things certainly did not go entirely according to plan. With the race only a couple of weeks away the engine was on the Plumstead test bed and going full-blast when the cast-iron crankshaft broke, and half the shaft with dynamometer coupling attached went whizzing round the test shop taking chunks out of the concrete pillars, while the test crew crouched low and covered their heads.

A replacement shaft – in steel, this time – was immediately put in hand, the bike was assembled and rushed over to the Isle of Man. Although Robin Sherry reported later that the vibration was wondrous to

From the right-hand side, one can see the relationship of the G45 timing case to that of its road-going G9 cousin.

Crankcase layout betrays the roadster origin of the Matchless G45 racer. It had a moderately-successful track career, notably in sidecar racing.

experience, he did at least run home in fourth place at 83.71 mph. From that autumn on, and throughout the winter, Ike Hatch and his team were busy, the result of their efforts being the very first G45 – still very recognisably G9-based, but now with the tank, seat and cycle parts of the 350 cc Model 7R racer, complete with the fat rear suspension units (the famous 'Jampots') of AMC's own design and manufacture. As far as the

Specification

Make Matchless *Model* G45

Capacity 498 cc	*Bore and stroke* 66 × 72.8 mm
Power output 48 bhp at	*Weight (dry)* 320 lb
7,200 rpm	*Price when new* £390 0s 0d
Wheelbase 55.5 in	

Tyre size: front 3.00 × 19 in; *rear* 3.50 × 19 in

Suspension: front Telescopic, oil-damped
rear Swinging-arm, with spring-and-hydraulic dampers

Manufacturer Associated Motor Cycles Ltd, 44 Plumstead Road, London SE18

engine was concerned, the main external departure from G9 practice was a new cylinder head on which the finning was carried up and around the front rocker box.

Once more the Manx Grand Prix would be the factory's proving ground – although this was against a background of disapproval from the large body of enthusiasts who contended that the TT Races were the proper place for works models, experimental or not; the Manx Grand Prix should be strictly for the amateur rider.

However, Matchless went ahead, this time with Derek Farrant as the rider, and in the 1952 Senior Manx GP Derek ran home as winner at 88.65 mph, having set a lap record of 89.64 mph; by a coincidence Bob McIntyre finished a good second on another AMC machine – a *three-fifty* Model 7R AJS! Encouraged by the Manx result, Plumstead lost no time in getting the G45 into production, and the new 1953-season racing twin was the proud centrepiece of the Matchless stand at the Earls Court Show a couple of months later.

New Zealander George Murphy rode the Matchless G45 twin in the 1953, 1954, and 1955 Senior TT races in the Isle of Man. Here he prepares for an evening practice run in 1955, though in the race mechanical trouble brought retirement after a second 46-minute lap.

Carburation was by a pair of Amal TT instruments fed by a single float chamber mounted between the two. The long intake bell is interesting.

Noteworthy were the massively-finned head, twin $1\frac{3}{32}$-in diameter Amal GP carburettors, and close-ratio Burman gearbox. An intriguing internal refinement was the use of roller-ended cam followers, the rollers running on needle-roller bearings.

In the next season or so the G45 was improved in various ways – a longer and higher fuel tank, indented at the rear for the rider's knees; a hump-back racing seat and rearset foot controls. Sadly, 1954 saw the death of the G45's designer and development engineer, Ike Hatch, but now Jack Williams was brought in, to carry on the good work.

The G45 was never intended to be anything more than a reliable second-level racer for the lads, and it was a role it fulfilled creditably on the short circuits and in the lesser meetings. Such was its popularity that no fewer than 17 of them took station on the Glencrutchery Road grid, for the start of the 1955 Senior TT. They were not disgraced, and in the face of the fully-fledged works teams the sixth place of Manxman Derek Ennett at 92.54 mph was highly creditable.

The G45 was a little less successful as a sidecar racing model, although Wolverhampton's Pip Harris persevered throughout the 1955 season, his haul including third in the Sidecar TT and fifth in the Belgian Grand Prix sidecar class.

It is a 1955-specification example of the G45 twin that is pictured here, and for that year there were a number of minor improvements such as a better shape of inlet tract and a compression ratio raised to 10 to 1, helping to produce an output of 48 bhp at 7,200 rpm. Other 1955 touches included improved braking, ignition by rotating-magnet Lucas magneto, and a twin-feed primary chain lubricator.

Nevertheless, the G45 was already on the way out,

and although it remained available until 1958 further development was minimal. The reason was that Associated Motor Cycles had decided to replace it with a single-cylinder model – the G50 which, because it used so many parts which were already in production for the 7R, was a more viable proposition. Performances of the twin and the new single were about the same (the G50 output was 47 bhp at 7,200 rpm) and for the racer-in-the-street owning a pair of models – 350 cc AJS and 500 cc Matchless – there was the enormous advantage that spares for one (except for pistons and rings) would fit the other, so there was less clutter in the workshop, and less to be carried to meetings.

In fact, possibly the only one to lose out by the switch was the race supporter. Pleasant though the boom of the big single might sound, it did not really compare with the harmony of a twin-exhaust twin on full throttle.

1958 Matchless 592 cc G11CSR Sports Twin

It might be said of the Matchless G11CSR that though its production life was a short one, it turned out to be unexpectedly adventurous! In fact the 592 cc Sports Twin (after a year in which it was sold exclusively in America) only came on to the British market in the autumn of 1958 – and by the following autumn it had gone, supplanted by the 650 cc G12 in its various guises.

As for the 'adventurous' bit, that was when sales director (and former works TT rider) Jock West cooked up a publicity stunt with *The Motor Cycle* technical editor, Vic Willoughby. Never before had a standard production roadster, fully dressed with silencer, registration plates and lights, had a go at the hundred-miles-in-an-hour game. So why not try it?

One big snag was that there was no really suitable race track in Britain where the attempt could be held; Montlhèry, near Paris, would have been ideal – but costly. The answer proved to be the Motor Industry Research Association's proving track at Lindley, near Nuneaton, which had high banked bends suitable for sustained high speeds. Except that MIRA was fully occupied almost all day long, with heavy lorries, bus chassis, and assorted vehicles of every nature all trundling or howling around, their drivers intent on fulfilling their own test programmes.

At only one period of any day was the track reasonably free of traffic: lunch hour, of course! Should the attempt fail then there was no chance of making adjustments and trying again. So preparations were made, the signal was given, Vic pressed his chin on to the pad atop the fuel tank – and round and round went the Matchless, obeying the signals given by the pit crew, until the official timekeepers gave the thumbs-up.

Top gear and wide-open throttle for 38 non-stop laps, and that was it – 102.926 miles in the level sixty minutes, using perhaps a pint of oil and three gallons of fuel, with the only damage a broken rear-lamp connection inside the bulb holder. Not only that but, as soon as the test was over, the Matchless technician rode it the hundred-plus miles back to the factory!

Like every other major factory, Matchless had followed the vertical-twin trend as soon as possible after the gruelling days of the Second World War, their contribution being the Phil Walker-designed 500 cc Model G9. But though 500 cc was perfectly adequate for British riders of the time, the Americans wanted more power, and still more power: Triumph enlarged their Speed Twin, to produce the 650 cc Thunderbird; BSA's A7 was joined by the 650 cc A10; the 497 cc Norton

Right: *fans called the CSR the 'Coffee Shop Racer'. However, the looks were more than skin-deep, for it had performance too!*

Below: *a flashy appearance counted for much among those who favoured the Matchless CSR models, hence the chromium-plated fork shrouds, rear damper covers, and tank side panels. Mudguards were in polished light alloy.*

Dominator 88 gave rise to the 597 cc Dominator 99; and so on, right along the line . . .

Matchless (and AJS, of course, for the two makes were mechanically identical) evolved the 592 cc Gll twin, but as the cry for still more performance rang out across the Atlantic Ocean, development engineer Jack Williams got to work. Modified inlet tracts and combustion chambers, a reshaping of the cams, compression ratio raised to 8.5 to 1, and a switch from separate exhaust pipes to a siamese system with single silencer well tucked in on the right of the model, all played a part in lifting power output from the 34 bhp of the original touring G11 introduced in 1956, to 39.5 bhp at 6,000 rpm from the new G11CSR Sports Twin. The frame, it was said, was based on that of the scrambler.

Indeed there were two hot newcomers to that 1958 range, the first being the short-wheelbase G11CS ('C' for 'Competition' and 'S' for 'Spring frame'), a street-scrambler to the American-market taste. The second model, the CSR (which in AMC parlance meant 'Competition, Spring frame, Roadster') was given a glamour finish with chromium-plated panels to the fuel tank, and polished light-alloy mudguards fore and aft with above-average wheel clearance. And whatever the

Breathing is looked after by a single Amal Monobloc carburettor. To give your Matchless an individual touch, you could have fitted an extended or even Perspex-fronted float chamber.

makers may have intended, the motor cycling public translated those CSR initials as meaning 'Coffee Shop Racer'!

By far the majority of Matchless twins were shipped over to the USA, and of course he who pays the piper calls the tune. The competitions version of the 592 cc twin, the G11CS, was performing well in the desert enduros of California – yet the Americans were still not satisfied. Their favourite expression was: 'There ain't no substitoot fer cubes', meaning that the more cubic inches of engine capacity available, the beefier the output.

However, 592 cc was just about as big as it was possible to take the original Phil Walker design, because of the limitations set by the distance between cylinder centres. The G11 had been produced simply by boring out the G9 cylinder block from 66 mm to 72 mm. The only other way the engine could be increased in size would be by lengthening the stroke (to 79.3 mm, as against 72.8 mm of the 592 cc model). That meant a new crankshaft and, in consequence, new crankcase castings in which to house it. And since the crankshaft was to be redesigned anyway, it was a good opportunity to lengthen the drive-side shaft so that a Lucas

Specification

Make Matchless *Model* G11CSR

Capacity 592 cc
Power output 33 bhp at
    6,800 rpm
Wheelbase 55.25 in
Tyre size: front 3.25 × 19 in; *rear* 3.50 × 19 in

Bore and stroke 72 × 72.8 mm
Weight (dry) 400 lb
Price when new £296 18s 0d

Suspension: front Telescopic, oil-damped
    rear Swinging-arm, with spring-and-hydraulic dampers

Manufacturer Associated Motor Cycles Ltd, 44 Plumstead Road, London SE18

alternator could be mounted on it, thus dispensing with need for the old-style separate magneto and direct-current dynamo electrics that had been employed ever since the twins came into the range.

Of 646 cc capacity and designated G12, the new and bigger model completely superseded the 592 cc G11, although the smaller 498 cc G9 twin remained in the catalogue. Indeed for 1959 there was a choice of four twins in each capacity – standard, de luxe, CS street scrambler, and CSR sports (essentially the scrambler decked out with roadgoing equipment). Except on the scrambler – which had fat tyres, high bars and a 2-gallon tank – the 1959 twins all featured a shapely 4.5-gallon fuel tank. The standard and de luxe models were fitted with mudguards of a deeper and more rounded contour than before.

From this point on, though, it was mainly downhill for the Matchless factory, the moment of truth for the shareholders arriving in 1961 when news broke that the previous year's profit of £219,000 had become a loss of £350,000. The range began to shrink, the first of the big models to get the chop being the 646 cc G12CS scrambler which had not been the success its makers had hoped for. By 1962 the smaller twins had gone, and only the standard G12 and sports twin G12CSR (renamed the Matchless Monarch, for no good reason) remained. As the firm sank deeper and deeper into the mire, so the programme became a bewilderment almost impossible to decipher, with Norton engines appearing in Matchless frames and, for all anyone knew, the other way about, too. It could not last, and in 1966 Matchless ceased to trade.

Almost against the odds, the name *did* survive for a couple of seasons more, under the new management of Norton-Villiers, but the programme was only a shadow of what had been.

Among the better features of the Matchless twin was the hefty cast-light-alloy primary chaincase, which at least was a vast improvement over the old-style pressed chaincase with alleged sealing band.

Splayed exhaust ports do not make for a very easy arrangement of a Siamese exhaust system. Width of the AMC vertical twin is explained by its adoption of a three-main-bearing crankshaft.

1955 Norton 497 cc Dominator 88

No motor cycle has ever caught the public's imagination as strongly as did Edward Turner's masterpiece, the 1937 Triumph Speed Twin – and of course, rival firms were not prepared to sit back and let Triumph get away with it. Had the Second World War not happened when it did, there would have been vertical-twins in abundance on the British market by late 1940. Panther, indeed, had already announced their twin (although, ironically, it was not brought back when peace did return); BSA were already running prototypes; and there were others in the pipeline.

But Hitler had other ideas, and so it was not until the war was out of the way that British motor cyclists could drool over a variety of vertical-twins from many makers.

Norton's contribution, announced in 1948, was the 497 cc Dominator – from the drawing board of Bert Hopwood who, in earlier days, had been Edward Turner's assistant. However, once the Dominator had gone into production Bert left Bracebridge Street in response to an urgent call from BSA; there, he designed the never-to-be-forgotten A10 Golden Flash twin. But by 1955 he was back at the Norton works, where the first fruit of the re-engagement was the Dominator 88 (followed for 1956 by the 597 cc version, the Dominator 99).

What was new about the 88 and 99 was that they employed the famous duplex-loop, all-welded frame which had proved so outstandingly successful in the road-racing field. Naturally, racing enthusiasts had taken particular note of the Manx Norton's featherbed frame and were eager to try its much-vaunted comfort for themselves. The 88 and 99 gave them the opportunity. In fact the frames of the racers were hand-built from expensive Reynolds 531 steel tubing, whereas production roadster frames employed A-grade commercial tubing. This was good enough for the purpose, of course, for a roadster frame does not have to withstand the severe stresses of cornering at racing speeds.

Incidentally, the first 88 and 99 had the so-called wideline frames, and with no fewer than 11.5 inches of seat nose and fuel tank between his thighs the smaller rider, especially, had a right to complain of lack of comfort. However, it would be 1960 before the top runs of the frame tubes would be cranked inward at the rear of the tank, to allow for a narrower, and far more comfortable, nose to the seat. It should be said, too, that the engine of the old-style Dominator 7 had a cast-iron

Specification

Make Norton *Model* Dominator 88

Capacity 497 cc
Power output 29.5 bhp at
   7,000 rpm
Wheelbase 55.5 in
Tyre size: front 3.00 × 19 in; *rear* 3.50 × 19 in

Bore and stroke 66 × 72.6 mm
Weight (dry) 380 lb
Price when new £280 1s 3d

Suspension: front Telescopic, oil-damped
           rear Swinging-arm, with spring-and-hydraulic dampers

Manufacturer Norton Motors Ltd, Bracebridge Street, Aston,
Birmingham 6

cylinder block and head. The new twins introduced the light-alloy head.

The year 1958 was significant for the design of the Dominator 88, because it marked a departure from previous Norton practice. Gone was the old arrangement of front-mounted separate dynamo and rear-mounted magneto, for now there was coil ignition, and a Lucas alternator carried on the engine drive shaft. However, to keep redesign work to the minimum the old magneto drive chain was retained, although now it drove a distributor unit which incorporated a bob-weight advance-and-retard mechanism.

The previous year, 1957, had seen the passing of an old tradition, the chromium-plated fuel tank that had graced the first featherbed Dommies. Nortons had found it cheaper – and almost as effective – to leave the tank in a painted condition but embellished with separate chromium-plated side panels framed in plastic beading. The mourners were joined by the sidecar fanatics, for the featherbed frame had no sidecar fixing points, nor were the manufacturers at all keen on condoning the fitting of a chair because of possible frame distortion.

During 1960, in addition to the slimline featherbed frame mentioned earlier, Nortons went into the realms of rear-wheel enclosure, once again following a fashion set by Triumph. However, fortunately, customers did not have to have the tinware-draped De Luxe Dominators: the standard undraped models remained in the catalogue (at £6 cheaper, what is more!).

Looking ahead a further year, racing department chief Doug Hele would instal a tuned 497 cc Dominator 88 engine in a genuine Manx racing frame and take it to the Isle of Man. There, in the 1961 Senior TT, Tom Phillis would make racing history by bringing the

Left: *Norton were justly proud of their robustly-built Roadholder telescopic front fork, though the ride it afforded was rather unyielding. Note also the separate pilot light slung under the headlamp, a fashion of the period.*

machine home third after lapping at over 100 mph. Race fans saw the model (nicknamed the Domiracer, what else?) as a logical successor to the illustrious but now rapidly being outclassed overhead-camshaft Manx single. That might indeed have come to pass, except that the AMC group which controlled the Norton works were heading towards bankruptcy.

In an attempt to cut their losses, they closed Bracebridge Street by 1962 and moved Norton production to the parent Plumstead works; the Domiracer had no part in AMC plans. Concentration of production failed to stave off disaster, and before long the entire AMC group had gone to the wall.

Yet the Dominator power unit was destined to survive the crash and soldier on – enlarged first to 750 cc, then to 850 cc and canted forward instead of sitting upright – as the heart of the Wolverhampton-built

Norton Commando of the 1970s. That, though, is another story.

Nevertheless, we should now look at the Dominator concept in greater detail. First of all, the engine has just a single camshaft, across the front, with all four light-alloy pushrods rising at a rearward-sloping angle between the two cylinders. Exhaust ports are splayed outward, to permit the maximum possible impact of cooling air upon the cylinder-head finning in the region of the ports.

The crankshaft is of three-piece construction, with the left and right crank throws bolted, through flanges, to the hefty centre flywheel. Connecting rods are light-alloy H-section forgings with steel-backed big-end bearings lined with micro-babbit wearing surfaces. In a way, a simple and straightforward design; but, as history was to prove, an exceptionally durable one.

Right: designer Bert Hopwood arranged for the exhaust ports to be splayed, to permit a greater supply of cooling air to reach the cylinder head. Pushrods, actuated by a single camshaft at the front, were housed in a sloping tunnel cast between the cylinders.

Far right: how the 'wideline' featherbed frame necessitated a wide-fronted dual seat can just be seen. Later, the frame tubes were brought closer together aft of the tank; this was the 'slimline' frame.

1962 Norton 499 cc Model 30M Manx

If just one machine had to be chosen to represent Britain at the very pinnacle of its road-racing glory, then beyond any argument it would have to be a Featherbed Manx Norton. The 'featherbed' tag was not mentioned in any Norton literature, although that was the name by which the post-war duplex-frame racer was known the world over. In fact it was an unofficial title which derived from the remark of old-timer Harold Daniell after riding one of the newly-introduced models in 1950. By comparison with the old brazed-lug-frame, sprung-heel Nortons (which again had an unofficial name among the cognoscenti, the Garden Gate models) it was, said Harold, like lying on a featherbed.

Oddly enough the famous frame was not designed at the Norton works, but was a private venture by Rex and Cromie McCandless, of Belfast, the brothers who were already widely-known among motor cycle enthusiasts for the Feridax-McCandless swinging-arm rear suspension conversion kits which could turn any pre-war hard-tail frame into something very much more comfortable. The McCandless brothers took their

prototype frame, built in Belfast with the unwitting assistance of the Short Aircraft factory, along to the Norton people in Bracebridge Street, Birmingham. Nortons liked it, and bought the idea.

Actually, the featherbed frame was outstanding for its simplicity. Each of the two main members was a complete tubular loop which began at the top of the steering head, passed downward, rearward, upward, and forward again to the base of the same steering head (so that in fact the two ends of each loop crossed, rearward of the head). Construction was all-welded, except that initially the rear sub-frame was bolted to the main section.

Later the sub-frame was welded-on, and for racing machines the tubing used was always high-tensile, chrome-molybdenum Reynolds 531, all joints being Sifbronze welded. In time the featherbed frame was used also on the roadster range, but since it was not subject to racing stresses Grade A tubing was substituted for Reynolds 531.

More a matter of evolution than design, the overhead-camshaft Norton engine, with its familiar bevel gear and vertical shaft drive to the cambox could be traced back to the early 1930s, when Arthur Carroll did a complete revamp of the CS1-type Walter Moore ohc engine (recognisable by the elongated blister housing the lower camshaft drive bevels), after the departure of Moore for the NSU factory in Germany.

The Manx name was not used in pre-war days, the production version of the works racer being sold (in 350 or 500 cc capacity, as required) as the Model 40 or Model 30 International to racing specification. By 1939, however, the as-sold Norton racer had moved

Without doubt the most succesful racing engine of its time, the Manx Norton put up a gallant rearguard action against the advance of the continental multi-cylinders.

Left: naked and unashamed, the Manx Norton was perhaps the most familiar of all racing machines on the tracks in the 1950s.

further and further from the International concept (as the name implies, the Inter was named for its performance in the International Six Days Trial), and was a Manx to all intents and purposes.

Works-entered 'Garden Gates' had telescopic forks and plunger rear springing in 1938, and when production was resumed after the war these features were found on the over-the-counter Manx racers, too.

Specification

Make Norton *Model* 30M Manx

Capacity 499 cc
Power output 47 bhp at
 6,500 rpm
Wheelbase 54.5 in
Tyre size: front 3.00 × 19 in; *rear* 3.50 × 19 in

Bore and stroke 86 × 85.8 mm
Weight (dry) 313 lb
Price when new £528 0s 0d

Suspension: front Telescopic, oil-damped
 rear Swinging-arm, with spring-and-hydraulic dampers

Manufacturer Norton Motors Ltd, Bracebridge Street, Aston, Birmingham 6

The first featherbeds were used by the factory racing team – Artie Bell, Johnny Lockett, Harold Daniell and a newcomer recruited from the Royal Signals Display Team, Geoffrey Duke – in 1950, and the early models featured a faired tail-cum-rear mudguard, aft of the seat.

After a wartime emigration to BSA, Joe Craig had returned to resume his role of race-shop chief, managing to wring every year another couple of horse-power from the same basic double-ohc racing engine. From 1950 Duke, in particular, brought off a fantastic run of successes which were to take him to a string of World Championship titles. Geoff had strong backing from his team-mates with Dublin's Reg Armstrong, particularly, always ready to step into the breech should anything happen to sideline the team leader. Indeed, it was Armstrong who was involved in the most incredible Senior TT victory of all time, in 1952.

From the start, battle was joined between the Norton pairing of Duke and Armstrong, and Les Graham on

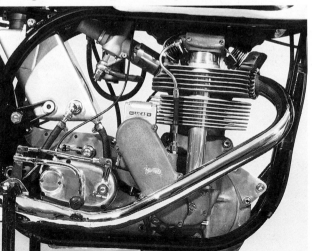

Left: the D-shape megaphone exhaust is deliberate, the flattened section permitting the rider to lean the machine that much further into a bend. The 350 cc versions were usually fitted with a reverse-cone megaphone to suit the different power characteristics.

Drive to the overhead camshaft is by vertical shaft, with bevel gearing top and bottom. The hairpin valve springs always did run exposed to the air.

The gear pedal linkage seen in this view was completely typical of the Manx Norton. Characteristic, too, is the rubber-band suspension of the oil tank.

the MV Agusta four, and for the first four laps Geoff Duke held the lead, with Graham second and Reg Armstrong third. And when Duke was forced to drop out with a burnt-out clutch, Reg was nicely placed to increase the pace and forge ahead of Les Graham into the lead.

Back at the Grandstand in Douglas, the note of the all-conquering Norton could be heard in the distance, then as the chequered flag swept down Reg throttled back and sat up – and at that moment the primary chain of the Norton snapped and fell into the roadway, right on the finish line. Talk about the Luck of the Irish! However, a couple of months later Reg Armstrong's primary chain again broke when he was in the lead. This time, though, he was 2.5 miles out, and the incident cost him the near-certainty of the 500 cc World Championship crown.

Overall, time was not on the side of that magnificent Norton engine, and the team had to struggle harder and

yet harder to maintain their place against the rapidly-improving continental challengers. Even Joe Craig eventually recognised that the Manx had come to the end of the line, and experiments were put in hand for a new racer – still a single, but with the engine lying horizontally in the manner of the Moto Guzzi. Long-term, there was to be a Norton four, but before anything more could be done the Norton factory announced, in 1955, that it would be withdrawing from Grand Prix racing. No longer needed as race shop supremo, Joe Craig retired at the end of the year and, sadly, he was to die in a car crash on the continent less than 18 months later.

Production of the Manx for private sale continued for several years more, but the numbers made grew fewer and fewer. The last batch of all was put in hand in 1962, the same year in which news was broken that the famous Bracebridge Street works were to be closed, as a consequence of the deepening financial troubles of the parent AMC group. The 1962 499 cc Manx pictured in these pages represents, therefore, the end of an era. Norton would live on, in the years ahead, but both the Manx, and Bracebridge Street itself, were dead.

1964 Panther 645 cc Model 120S

There must have been some special quality in the Bradford air which bred a sturdy independence in thought, when it came to designing a motor cycle. There was, for example, Alfred Angas Scott and his water-cooled two-stroke twins; and there was also, from nearby Cleckheaton, Joah Carver Phelon who hit upon the idea of employing the engine as an integral part of the frame structure, in place of the conventional frame front down tube.

His first motor cycle employing the principle was built as long ago as 1900. And the scheme was such a sound one that it was still in use when the final batch of 645 cc Model 120 singles was sold off in 1966.

Yes, indeed; a 645 cc single, with 88 mm bore and a fantastic 'one bang every second lamp post' stroke of 106 mm. That was the Model 120, essentially for the sidecar man hauling a double-adult family saloon; upon its introduction in 1959 the press of the day remarked that it was 'The Biggest Aspidistra in the World – and All in One Pot!' Underlining the fact that the makers considered it a sidecar haulier, the front fork was set-up for sidecar use, and should there be anyone brave enough to want to ride it solo the works would provide a special fork yoke to alter the trail, and a set of solo gears.

Simultaneously with the announcement of the Model 120, Panthers unveiled a special sidecar chassis, so tailored that it could be bolted directly to the bike, saving all the usual messing about with adjustable fittings to obtain the correct amount of lean-out and toe-in. Not only that, but the sprung sidecar wheel was interchangeable with either of the machine wheels, so that a spare wheel (optional, as was the spare wheel

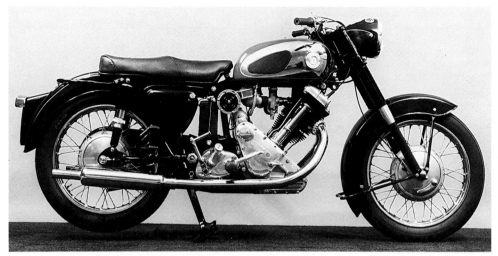

carrier) could be mounted on the sidecar body.

So confident were the manufacturers of the machine's phenomenal pulling power that the rectangular-shape tubular chassis even embodied a towing eye, to which a trailer could be attached!

Ancestor of this biggest 'pussy' of them all had been the 490 cc Redwing 100, brought into the range as long ago as 1932, and gradually developed over the years (there was nothing hasty about the Panther folk!). An adjustment of bore and stroke dimensions brought the capacity to 598 cc (87 × 100 mm) in the late 1930s, and around 1938–39 the model reached a peak, with totally enclosed valve gear but still, at this stage, the traditional girder front fork and rigid frame. On its return to the market in 1946, it was virtually unaltered from pre-war times, but modernity caught up in 1947, when a Dowty air-sprung telescopic fork was adopted;

Above: *the Phelon & Moore concept of employing the engine in place of the frame front down tube dates from the turn of the century when it was employed also (under P & M licence) by Humber.*

Right: *so thoroughly sidecar-oriented was the 645 cc Panther Model 120, that a customer requiring one for solo use had to order specially. Almost at the end of the line, this 1964 example was built under the eye of the Official Receiver.*

in time there would be, too, swinging-arm rear suspension.

But now there was competition in the sidecar-haulage field from the 650 cc vertical twins offered by BSA and Triumph. Therefore during 1958 the Cleckheaton factory developed a 650 cc of their own – a single, naturally, and no speedster but a bike with low-down torque in abundance. It was achieved by increasing the bore by just 1 mm, and employing an entirely new crankshaft which gave a 6 mm increase in stroke, running on larger-diameter Ransomes & Marles ball main bearings. Nor was it only a matter of enlargement, for a smaller exhaust valve, squish-band combustion chamber, and bigger Amal carburettor, ensured that the power output was the product of solid beef. Distinguishing the new Model 120 from its smaller Model 100 sister (which continued in production) was a chromium-plated fuel tank, with a silver-grey top face. Price on introduction in the 1959 Panther range was £258 17s 0d.

Initial sales were quite good, but purchasers were to find that there were a number of teething problems (the Burman clutch, for one, objected to the extra load it now had to handle) and oil consumption was on the heavy side. Improvements were made, but as the

Because the Panther 120 was almost invariably used for sidecar work, rear fork construction had to be particularly massive. The damper units are of Armstrong manufacture.

Very long studs, passing right through to the main bearing area of the crankcase, ensure that the frame stresses are properly distributed.

Specification

Make Panther *Model* 120S

Capacity 645 cc	*Bore and stroke* 88 × 106 mm
Power output Not recorded	*Weight (dry)* 462 lb
Wheelbase 57 in	*Price when new* £279 0s 0d

Tyre size: front 3.50 × 19 in; *rear* 3.50 × 19 in

Suspension: front Telescopic, oil-damped
           rear Swinging-arm, with spring-and-hydraulic dampers

Manufacturer Phelon & Moore Ltd, Cleckheaton, Bradford, Yorkshire

machine ran on into the 1960s it was evident that its old-fashioned design was being left far behind. Where rival makers had long adopted unit-construction and alternator electrics, the big Panther still adhered to a separate gearbox, and 'ye olde' Lucas Magdyno – until, eventually, it was the last bike in the world to be so equipped.

With Burman's main customer, Ariel, no longer making big four-strokes, that firm now proposed to drop motor cycle gearbox manufacture completely, and devote their factory to the high-volume production of steering gear for British Leyland cars. And Lucas were to make it a double blow, for the Magdyno was being phased out and Panthers would need to adapt (as did Velocette) to some other form of ignition.

There was yet another factor to be considered, for Panther's traditional sidecar-driver customer was fast losing faith, wooed away from three wheels to four by vehicles such as the BL Mini. By 1962, Panthers were in the hands of the Official Receiver, although manufacture was to continue at a lower rate of production right up to 1966, using such stocks of Lucas Magdynos and Burman gearboxes as they had been able to call back from dealers – or rather, dealer, for by this time production of the big singles was being channelled through one outlet only, George Clarke Motors, of Brixton.

For the final batch, sold off by George Clarke at suicide prices, it was said that the works had had to resort to the use of reconditioned second-hand gearboxes and Magdynos. Had the financial situation been healthier, the Big Pussy might have purred on for a little while more. Even under Official Receivership the works had been developing a more modern Model 120, with crankshaft mounted alternator and 12-volt electrical system, and with an AMC gearbox – costly, but there was no other option open – replacing the familiar Burman. But it was a dream fated never to come true.

Dating from 1964, the 645 cc Model 120 pictured in these pages is the machine in its ultimate stage of development, built at a time when the shadow hovering over Cleckheaton was growing steadily blacker, and hope was fast being abandoned. It was a bike of its time, but that time had long gone by.

Panther were the very last firm to build a twin-port ohv single, though to assist in mounting a sidecar on the left a single-port head could be supplied.

1951 Royal Enfield 496 cc 500 Twin

On the whole, the Royal Enfield people were rather good at thinking up attractive names for their machines – like Bullet, Crusader, Clipper, Super Meteor, and Constellation. So it was rather surprising that their 496 cc vertical-twin should have been listed as the pure and simple '500 Twin' throughout its production life, which ran from 1949 to 1957. There was still a 500 cc twin in the range from 1958 onward, but that was the Meteor Minor, a complete redesign with fatter bore, shorter stroke, and a bigger helping of power output.

What we are concerned with here is the original 500 Twin as introduced in November 1948. The work of Ted Pardoe and Tony Wilson-Jones, it was unlike the vertical-twins now emerging from other British factories in that there were two independent cast-iron barrels, each with its own light-alloy cylinder head and integral rocker box. The skirts of the cylinder barrels were sunk very deeply indeed – in fact by over half their length – into the mouth of the high crankcase assembly.

To a considerable extent the new twin followed existing Royal Enfield design practice. There was, for instance, the familiar arrangement of an oil compartment cast into the crankcase assembly. Familiar, too, was the double-ended oil pump embodied in the base of the timing cover and driven by a worm on the end of the crankshaft. The frame was very similar to that of the single-cylinder Bullet, and incorporated the swinging-arm suspension system of which Royal Enfield had been post-war pioneers. At this stage proprietary spring-damper units, such as those by Girling or Armstrong, had yet to put in an appearance, and so the Redditch-based factory had to design and make their own short units. The front fork, too, was Royal Enfield's own and, unusually, carried the front wheel spindle ahead of the centre-line of the fork; the upper fork crown embodied a very neat central housing for the speedometer.

In essence, the engine was a double-up of the 248 cc single-cylinder Model S and used the same bore and stroke dimension of 64 × 77 mm. The crankshaft, however, was something special for it was a one-piece alloy-iron casting with integral centre flywheel. There were no big-end or little-end bearings as such, for the light-alloy connecting rods ran direct on the crank throws, while the gudgeon pins operated in the unbushed little-end eye. Inlet and exhaust camshafts were carried high in the crankcase assembly and were disposed behind and ahead of the cylinders – an arrangement which facilitated the use of short pushrods.

Though the Royal Enfield 500 Twin looks a docile tourer, in fact it had a distinguished sporting background. Representing the factory, a trio of twins all gained gold medals in the 1961 ISDT in Italy.

The generous timing chest houses an endless chain driving the camshafts and Magdyno; the base of the timing cover embodies a double-ended oil pump driven by worm-wheel from the crankshaft end.

Timing gear was by chain, adjustment being made with the aid of a jockey sprocket mounted on an eccentric spindle; a separate short chain from the inlet camshaft drove a special direct-current dynamo on which the distributor was mounted vertically and driven from the dynamo shaft by skew gearing at a two-to-one ratio. Ignition was coil, of course.

Appearance of the engine/gearbox assembly was unit-construction, although in truth the four-speed Albion gearbox (which featured the usual Royal Enfield gimmick of a small, auxiliary neutral-finder pedal) was bolted directly to a flat vertical facing at the rear of the crankcase assembly. Conceived as a quiet and docile tourer, it had an initial compression ratio of only 6.5 to 1, and an inoffensive power output of 25 bhp at 5,500 rpm.

In its original form the Twin had an all-over livery of battleship grey, and a valanced front mudguard which did not rise and fall with the wheel. The 1950 version saw a switch to a most attractive silver grey with chromium-plated tank and red-outlined silver side and top panels, but there were no material changes until the 1951 version – as illustrated here – was announced. An encouraging customer response meant that the makers could now go to the expense of employing die-cast crankcases, fork-end design was changed, and for the first time the front mudguard was unsprung. Several pounds had been chopped from the weight, which was now down to a commendable 390 lb, dry.

Both of the weekly motor cycle magazines road-tested the 1951 500 Twin favourably, although *The Motor Cycle's* tester thought that a slightly narrower fuel tank would have added to rider comfort on long runs; he found, too, that the prop stand broke at the welding during the test, and the centre stand was awkward to use. Top speed was 85 or 86 mph, according to which magazine you read, but both agreed that the bike was undergeared.

Strangely enough, although its designers had never intended the Twin as a competitions mount, 1951 saw the machine acquit itself very well in what was always regarded as the toughest of all tests, the International Six Days Trial. That year the event took place in

Royal Enfield's first contribution to the vertical twin movement, the 500 Twin was a well-balanced design with much in its favour.

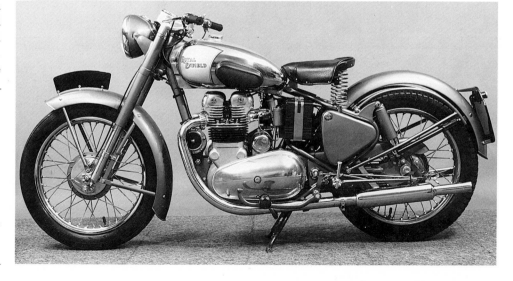

Specification

Make Royal Enfield *Model* 500 Twin

Capacity 496 cc	*Bore and stroke* 64 × 76 mm
Power output 25 bhp at 5,500 rpm	*Weight (dry)* 394 lb
	Price when new £212 14s 6d
Wheelbase 54 in	

Tyre size: front 3.25 × 19 in; *rear* 3.50 × 19 in

Suspension: front Telescopic, oil-damped
           rear Swinging-arm, with spring-and-hydraulic dampers

Manufacturer The Enfield Cycle Co Ltd, Hewell Road, Redditch, Worcestershire

Northern Italy, and because the British motor cycle industry was at this time pushing sales of its various vertical-twins in overseas markets, the Auto Cycle Union felt that the country's official ISDT teams should show faith in the product by campaigning twins, too.

Accordingly, three Twins were put into Six Days trim for the ACU selection tests, held in mid-Wales, and one of the Royal Enfield men – 'Jolly Jack' Stocker (in later years the British team manager) – was chosen for the British Trophy team. Encouraged, Royal Enfield mounted their own factory team on Twins, with Stan Holmes and young Johnny Brittain joining Jack Stocker to represent Redditch.

All three Twins acquitted themselves nobly, although it has to be admitted that there came an anxious moment during the speed test which ended the event, when Stan Holmes's model blew a gasket. But thanks to the separate-cylinder-head design, Stan was able to continue at only slightly diminished speed, to claim his gold medal.

By 1952, however, a bigger Royal Enfield (the 692 cc

Meteor) had joined the range, somewhat stealing the 500 Twin's thunder, although John Brittain and Don Evans used a couple as Vase team members in the 1952 ISDT. Gradually, the 500 slipped out of the limelight, although there were still a number of improvements to come in the years ahead (including, for its final production year of 1957, an all-welded frame and alternator electrics).

The 1958 replacement, the 496 cc Meteor Minor, had a compression ratio of 8 to 1, and a power output upped by 5 bhp. Certainly it was a livelier model than its forerunner, but there were still plenty who would have preferred the more leisurely charms of the 500 Twin.

79

1958 Royal Enfield 346 cc Clipper Airflow

It could just be that somebody in the Royal Enfield sales office was possessed of a wicked sense of humour. The Clipper, as a name, is evocative of tall ships under full sail racing home under blue skies and carrying precious cargoes; however, the truth was that Royal Enfield traditionally reserved the Clipper designation for the cheapest machine in the range, the one on which the frills and fancies had been 'clipped' so that it could be offered to the public at a bargain price.

Usually it looked just a bit outdated, which was hardly surprising because the Clipper was a means of using up surplus components, the leftovers from machines which had either been discontinued or revamped. Typical was the Clipper of the 1957 Royal Enfield programme, which was essentially a bargain-basement version of the old 346 cc Model G, but when the 1958 range was announced it was seen that the '350 Clipper' name had been transferred to something which was a sort of poor relation of the sporty Bullet.

Certainly the frame was pure Bullet, with single front down tube and twin rear loops, along with a pivoted rear fork controlled by Armstrong suspension units. In basic trim, the Clipper's front fork was typically Royal Enfield, topped by the familiar cast-light-alloy 'casquette' assembly housing the headlamp unit, speedometer, and two small pilot lamps; however, the front wheel used the full-width hub (with 6 in-diameter brake) of the 250 cc Crusader family. Unlike that of the more expensive Bullet, the rear wheel was non-quickly-detachable, and was not full-width but used the old-style single-sided brake drum – an example of the Redditch firm's canniness in using-up deleted parts from other models.

The 346 cc (70 × 90 mm bore and stroke) overhead-valve engine followed Bullet practice in most respects, although the cylinder and head were cast-iron. As in the Bullet, the connecting rod was of RR56 light alloy and – a Royal Enfield peculiarity that had been

Royal Enfield were pioneers in the use of glass-fibre for fairings and mudguards. The Airflow fairing was not a derivative of racing practice, but the post-1957 adoption of dolphin-type fairings in racing did lead to a demand for similar fairings for road use.

The Clipper was the cheaper version of the unit-construction Crusader, but could be supplied to special order with full Airflow fairing and front mudguard as seen here.

employed ever since 1939 – the big-end bearing was actually a stêel bush, coated with white metal inside and out and free to float within the big-end eye and on the crankpin. The bush contained evenly-spaced holes connected to a circumferential groove to allow for oil distribution. Typical of the factory's practice, the gudgeon pin ran directly in the little-end eye of the alloy con-rod, without the benefit of a bearing bush.

As with all Royal Enfield four-strokes of post-war years, the oil was carried in an extension of the crankcase, and a double-ended oil pump of oscillating-plunger type was incorporated in the timing cover. Most oilways were internal, and the only external piping was that from the timing chest to the rocker gear.

For the first time, the 1958 Clipper featured a Lucas 60-watt alternator housed within the cast-light-alloy primary chaincase, the rotor being carried on the drive-side engine shaft. Occupying the position, rearward of the cylinder, of the former Lucas Magdyno unit was a horizontally-mounted distributor driven by the timing gear, and the ignition coil. Power unit appearance was unit-construction, but actually the four-speed Albion gearbox was bolted directly to a vertical facing at the

The engine-gear unit is clearly a member of the Ted Pardoe-designed Crusader family. Oil is carried in a compartment of the crankcase, the filler cap being situated just aft of the cylinder barrel.

rear of the crankcase. Overall ratios were 5.67, 7.37, 10.2 and 15.8 to 1, and a small neutral-finding pedal – easily worked by a dab of the heel – operated from each ratio except bottom gear. Ensuring smooth transmission was the famous Royal Enfield cush-drive rear hub, in which the rear sprocket was coupled to the wheel by vanes inserted between rubber blocks.

As ever, the Clipper customer had to expect a utility finish for his money, and so chromium plating was cut to the minimum. The whole frame, mudguards and tank were painted black, although the sides of the 3-gallon tank were relieved by gold lining (and by a rather ugly plated pressed-steel-winged embellishment, a version of which would be used many years later by Enfield India). Looked upon as rather cheapjack at the time – although present-day restorers would give their right arms to find a cache in original state – was the fitting of a Terry sprung single saddle instead of a dualseat, but a dualseat could be supplied at extra cost. Cheapjack, too, was the old-style barrel silencer, the true Bullet

Specification

Make Royal Enfield *Model* Clipper Airflow

Capacity 346 cc
Power output 18 bhp at 5,750 rpm
Wheelbase 54 in
Tyre size: front 3.25 × 19 in; *rear* 3.25 × 19 in

Bore and stroke 70 × 90 mm
Weight (dry) 350 lb
Price when new £225 0s 0d

Suspension: front Telescopic, oil-damped
         rear Swinging-arm, with spring-and-hydraulic dampers

Manufacturer The Enfield Cycle Co Ltd, Hewell Road, Redditch, Worcestershire

Most unusually, the pushrods and timing gear are located on the primary drive side of the engine, though this is not immediately evident.

being provided with a better-styled and longer silencer with polished, light-alloy tail cap. Power output was a relatively inoffensive 16.5 bhp at 5,500 rpm, and total weight was 362 lb, quite heavy for a late 1950s three-fifty.

So far we have been describing the basic Clipper, but in fact the model displayed here is the slightly more expensive Clipper Airflow, which means that it came off the assembly line complete with the firm's own individually-styled glass-fibre fairing. Only two British factories took the trouble to market machines with tailored-to-suit fairings: Velocette with their Veeline-faired models; and Royal Enfield with their Airflow fairing. It should be said that the Redditch people were pioneers in this field, having co-operated with *The Motor Cycle* and technical artist Lawrie Watts in producing the one-off Dreamliner of 1956, the world's first motor cycle to be fitted with a properly designed glass-fibre fairing.

A traditional and much appreciated Royal Enfield feature was that the entire rear mudguard and seat assembly could be lifted clear, to give access to the rear tyre for maintenance purposes.

Spectacular as it was, the Dreamliner (which was just a 350 cc Royal Enfield Bullet, underneath) was primarily a design exercise, with full front dustbin fairing (incorporating twin headlamps) and stream-lined tail, it was too over-the-top for commercial production. The Airflow, however, was a more acceptable alternative. It incorporated headlamp mounting, legshields, and windscreen, and although it was designed for the very practical purpose of protecting the rider from wind and weather it came on the scene at just about the time that full dustbin fairings had been outlawed (from the 1958 season onward) from the race circuits in favour of the dolphin-type fairing which left the front wheel exposed.

The growing popularity of the dolphin for racing gave Royal Enfield's Airflow an unexpected boost. No longer would a rider whose machine sported legshields be considered 'cissy' by his mates. After all, fairings were used in the Isle of Man TT Races . . .

1947 Sunbeam 487 cc Model S7

In the years between the two great world wars, no motor cycle was more respected than the John Marston Sunbeam. Particularly, it was renowned for the deep gloss of its black enamel (John Marston had started in business as a Japan-enameller in Victorian times) but by the mid-1930s it had to be admitted that in mechanical development the Sunbeam lagged behind.

Manufacturing rights were acquired by Associated Motor Cycles, of Plumstead, already the manufacturers of Matchless and AJS. However, AMC had really bought Sunbeam for its bicycle know-how, and for the secret of that deep black finish; the motor cycle side was rather an embarrassment. Yet, after a year or two of assembling Sunbeams at Plumstead from existing stocks of Wolverhampton-made parts, an entirely new Sunbeam range of high-camshaft singles was introduced in 1938. But, the new Sunbeams had scarce enough time to gain market acceptance before the Second World War brought production to an end. However, in the closing months of hostilities Sunbeam advertisements began to reappear, hinting at the marvellous new model that would greet the return to peacetime riding. The big surprise, though, was the address at the foot of the advertisements – 'Sunbeam Motor Cycles, Armoury Road, Birmingham'. To anyone with a knowledge of the motor cycle world, this told its own story: the Sunbeam name had changed hands again, and was now in the BSA fold.

In due course the promised new Sunbeam appeared in the journals of the day, and it was hailed as really something! Sitting on great, fat tyres (4.75 × 16 in), it was a sleek heavyweight powered by an all-alloy, in-line, overhead camshaft twin, with the gearbox built in

unit, and shaft final drive. Front suspension was by a massive telescopic fork with separate spring box carried between the two fork stanchions, and rider comfort was aided by a cantilever saddle with

Right: *designer of the postwar in-line Sunbeam, Erling Poppe was greatly influenced by the BMW layout, and certainly the front fork and cantilever saddle have Teutonic overtones.*

Left: *the power unit is an in-line overhead-camshaft twin carried from the frame by rubber mountings. Details to note are the front-mounted pancake direct-current dynamo, and the streamlined cover over the side-mounted carburettor.*

compensated springing system in which the springs were housed within the frame.

The designer was Erling Poppe, who in the 1920s had been a partner with Gilmour Packman in the ill-fated P & P motor cycle concern; latterly, though, he had been involved in lorry engine design at Dennis Brothers, so his return to the motor cycle field was a surprise. Although it was not admitted at the time, the new Sunbeam was very much influenced by the wartime BMW (a captured example of which had been taken to the BSA works) while the Sunbeam engine had its inspiration in a BSA design – built to prototype stage, but never produced – known as the In-line Twin.

Manufacture of the new Sunbeam would not be undertaken at the main BSA works at Small Heath, however, but at the branch works at Redditch which, in earlier times, had built such famous models as the 250 cc 'Round Tank' and the 493 cc Sloper (later Redditch also produced the Bantam engine-gear units).

During the prototype test period, the new 487 cc Sunbeam was installed in a frame which lacked rear springing, but for production this was modified to plunger-type suspension. At first, too, the engine was bolted rigidly to the duplex frame and this did reach

Drive to the single overhead camshaft was by chain at the rear of the cylinder block. The distributor is driven by the rear end of the camshaft.

production; it was, though, a very serious mistake, for the first batch of S7 Sunbeams was rushed through so that they could be shipped out to South Africa, there to form a prestige escort during a Royal visit.

On arrival, they were found to vibrate so badly as to be almost unrideable, and the whole consignment had to be returned post-haste to Redditch for modification. The modification took the form of rubber mountings at each side of the fore part of the crankcase, plus a big rubber mounting at top front of the unit. Certainly this cured the vibration trouble, for now the engine could shake to its heart's content without affecting the frame. But there was a price to be paid, for it became necessary to insert a short length of flexible piping into the exhaust system, and this piece of bodging (which tended to rust and rot) remained part of the Sunbeam specification to the end of the model's production.

There was one other major clanger to rectify which would have required redesign, and BSA were not prepared to go to that extreme. Unlike the BMW, which employed bevel drive to the rear crownwheel, the Sunbeam opted for worm drive and it was soon discovered that this system could cope with only a limited amount of power; try to push more through, and

Specification

Make Sunbeam *Model* S7

Capacity 487 cc
Power output 24 bhp at
   6,000 rpm
Wheelbase 57 in
Tyre size: front 4.50 × 16 in; *rear* 4.75 × 16 in

Bore and stroke 70 × 63.5 mm
Weight (dry) 430 lb
Price when new £285 4s 0d

Suspension: front Telescopic, oil-damped
        rear Plunger (telescopic), undamped

Manufacturer Sunbeam Cycles Ltd, Armoury Road, Small Heath, Birmingham 11

the bronze worm (which, even on the mildly-tuned tourer, grew very hot in use) would wear out within a few hundred miles.

And so the super-sports engine, with 90-degree valve arrangement, which Sunbeam had intended to offer as an alternative to the luxury tourer had to be shelved.

There was no doubt whatever that the S7 was a majestic-looking motor cycle, but many thought that it was heavier than it actually was, and so the makers decided to issue a supplementary model – which looked a lot lighter and was, by 30 lb! This was the S8, in which the principal differences were the use of a BSA A10-type front fork and wheel, and tyres of more orthodox size. There was a difference, also, in the silencer, which on the S8 was an old-fashioned lozenge in cast light-alloy, instead of the S7's tapered tubular barrel.

Certainly the S7 and S8 found a coterie of admirers who enjoyed the more leisurely type of gentlemanly touring, but the customers were not sufficiently numerous to make the machine a marketable pro-position, and in 1957 the Sunbeam plant closed down. A close study of the design of the 1957 Sunbeam S7 – its final form – is very worthwhile. Immediately noticeable is the automobile influence

on engine construction, for the cylinder block and crankcase are one single light-alloy casting, the sump being a simple unstressed casting bolted to the underside. Housed in the cylinder head, the camshaft is driven by a chain at the rear of the unit. The forward end of the engine shaft drives a pancake-type direct-current dynamo, while the car-type ignition distributor is at the rear of the cylinder head, where it is driven by the camshaft. Attached to the rear of the engine, the gearbox is driven through a conventional single-plate Borg & Beck car clutch.

In its production span, the S7 Sunbeam was not modified very much, although the old-type inverted control levers were discarded from 1950, at which time also the front fork springs were housed within the stanchions. In 1952, an improved method of tensioning the camshaft drive chain was adopted as well as a new oil-pressure switch. But that was just about all, and when the 1957 season brought the final curtain, the audience had very largely already left the hall!

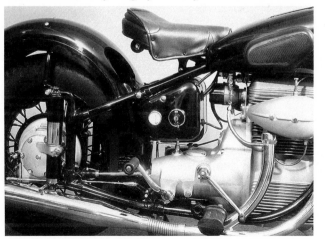

The short final-drive shaft was exposed, with a universal joint at each end. The underslung-worm drive at the rear wheel was a grave limit on the amount of power that could be transmitted.

On early Sunbeam twins the spring of the cantilever saddle was hidden within the frame top tube, and was actuated by a bell-crank lever.

1951 Triumph 498 cc TR5 Trophy

Triumph's remarkable all-rounder acquired its name by way of tribute to the men who, in 1948, had brought the prestigious International Trophy back to Britain by their success in that year's International Six Days Trial. In fact, Britain had just about cleared the board, for the squad had won, also, the International Vase, while the Triumph factory trio of veteran Allan Jefferies, Jimmy Alves, and Bert Gaymer all finished with clean sheets, to give Meriden one of the only two maker's team awards; the other team award went to Jawa of Czechoslovakia.

For Allan Jefferies (one of the best Six Days Trial men ever) and for Gaymer and Alves, the factory devised an extremely light 500 cc twin – only 304 lb, complete with lighting equipment, and the necessary spare footrests, compressed-air bottle, tyre levers and other essentials taped in place. It was, too, soft-tuned so that its power characteristics were more than usually flexible. The engines were basically Speed Twins, but with the silicon-alloy cylinder block that had been developed in wartime for a military generator plant.

It did not take Triumph long to cash-in on the spirit of euphoria generated by Britain's overwhelming success, and the brand-new TR5 Trophy had pride of place on the company's stand at the 1948 Earls Court Show. The new Grand Prix racer, too, made use of the generator-engine's square-finned cylinder block and head, but for the TR5 only a single carburettor was employed. Bottom-end assembly was pure Tiger 100 sports roadster, except the cams had a milder profile, and the engine and gearbox were slotted into a short-wheelbase (53-in) frame with ample ground clearance.

Today we would call it a trail bike, for it was bred for the mountain tracks, but in fact it was the most versatile and sweet-tempered bike ever to wear a Triumph badge. The factory offered a wide variety of camshafts, pistons and gear ratios; the engine was simple to work on in the home workshop. In consequence the average clubman could, and did, use his TR5 Trophy as home-to-work transport during the week, ride to a grass-track, scramble, sand-race, trial, or even short circuit road race, take off the headlamp and compete with a good chance of success. Then on would go the headlamp for the ride back home. But of course, motor cycle sport in the heady days of the immediate post-war period was far less specialised than it is today; it was also a lot more fun!

Initially the TR5 used the sand-cast head and barrel

Right: they called the TR5 Trophy 'the last of the all-rounders', and its demise was largely the result of a growing specialisation in motor cycle competitions.

Below: cobby and purposeful, the TR5 Trophy was an all-purpose competitions machine equally at home on the road or the rough. It gained its name as the result of British team success in the ISDT.

Specification

Make Triumph *Model* TR5 Trophy

Capacity 498 cc
Power output 25 bhp at
   6,000 rpm
Wheelbase 53 in
Tyre size: front 3.00 × 20 in; *rear* 4.00 × 19 in

Bore and stroke 63 × 80 mm
Weight (dry) 304 lb
Price when new £200 13s 3d

Suspension: front Telescopic, oil-damped
               rear Sprung hub

Manufacturer Triumph Engineering Co Ltd, Meriden Works,
Allesley, Coventry

(still with the little cast-in bosses within the fins which, when drilled and tapped, held the cooling-air ducting of the stationary generator engine) but for 1951 there was a change to a close-finned die-cast barrel, and this is the form taken by the machine displayed here.

The frame was still light and unsprung, for trials riders of the period felt that a sprung heel somehow lessened the directness of the drive between engine and rear wheel and induced wheelspin in slippery conditions. To promote sales of the twins, the Meriden factory's bread and butter, the works trials team were TR5-mounted. It is worth pointing out, also, that around this time the Triumph factory started to manufacture a side-valve vertical-twin, the Model TRW, for military service, and for expediency they used the rigid frame, tank (but painted instead of chromed) and cycle parts of the TR5 Trophy.

Of course, if a rider still insisted on having rear springing, he could fit his Trophy with Edward Turner's ingenious rear sprung hub. But not even the TR5 could stand in the way of progress, and so from 1955 onward the old rigid frame was discarded, and the Trophy adopted swinging-arm rear springing. By that time, in any case, the heyday of the all-things-to-all-men motor cycle was passing, and even the works trials team had switched to using Tiger Cubs.

Meanwhile, the expanding American market had discovered the delights of cross-country motor cycling – and with the vast open deserts in which to play, they demanded power and yet more power. The TR5 tried to oblige, by abandoning its soft-tuned camshaft and raising its compression ratio (there was even a high-rise handlebar) but it still was not enough for Transatlantic tastes, and so the 650 cc TR6 Trophy entered the range. Totally eclipsed by the newcomer, the old TR5 went into decline, and by 1958 it had

Left: after 1951, the original sand-cast cylinder block was replaced by a die-cast block with fine, close-pitched finning.

Right: a well-tucked-in, high-level siamese exhaust system was originally provided so that deep streams could be forded.

the bike between his knees, when picking his way across a boulder-strewn gully. And just a single saddle and mudguard pad, because although the TR5 rider *could* take a passenger, if pressed, this was really a machine for the loner.

In its prime years, the Trophy carried on its tank sides just the simple Triumph motif, eschewing the horizontal bands, or the space-ship badges of its road-going sisters. Just a plain tank, smart in chromium plate with blue-outlined silver panels in most years; but in the 1951–52 period came a world shortage of nickel and, thereafter, the Trophy had to make do with a tank of all-over silver. Serviceable, agreed, but somehow the glamour had been dimmed.

It is appropriate, therefore, that we should remember the TR5 Trophy as it stood in 1951, with three years of ISDT Team success behind it and at the height of its fame. From that point on, it was an anti-climax.

Right: though Edward Turner's famous Sprung Hub afforded only limited movement, it did mean that Triumph could continue to use their old rigid frame jigs. The Sprung Hub was an extra on everything except the 350 cc 3T twin.

disappeared, a victim of changing circumstances.

Look hard and long at our 1951 example, for this was what club motor cycling was all about. The front and rear mudguards have not been bobbed by some enterprising owner; that is exactly how the TR5 left the factory, and the shortened and raised guards were a precaution against their becoming clogged with mud when following forest trails.

Siamese exhausts were used for lightness, running at high level so that streams could be forded, and tucked well in against the side of the machine, to allow freedom for the rider to stand on the footrests and sway

1975 Triumph 987 cc Quadrant

There never was a production four-cylinder Triumph; even if there had been, the chances are that it would not have looked like the one-and-only prototype that is one of the proudest possessions of the National Motorcycle Museum collection. The machine never did have an official name, but since it was a logical extension of the Triumph Trident three-cylinder model, 'Quadrant' seemed to be an appropriate nickname.

The date is significant, for the machine was neither a product of Meriden, nor of the BSA Group research and development centre at Umberslade Hall. In fact, by the early 1970s the crashed BSA-Triumph empire had suffered a shotgun marriage with Norton-Villiers, to form NVT under the direction of Dennis Poore. Part of the NVT organisation was a sales and publicity subsidiary known as Norton Triumph International, based at Kitts Green, adjacent to Birmingham Airport. And it was in a small workshop to the rear of the main office block at Kitts Green that former Triumph development chief Doug Hele, and a selected band of workers drawn mainly from the old Daytona race-preparation shop at Meriden, set up business.

Their brief was to investigate a number of options that, hopefully, could take NVT into the future; and it was inevitable that the options would include a four. Money was so tight as to be almost non-existent, yet it was essential that a four-cylinder should be built – if only to prove that it was feasible. The only answer for Doug Hele and his merry men was to use as much of the existing Trident as was possible.

Because of the nature of its construction, much of the engine hangs out to the offside. It would have been redesigned, had production been contemplated.

Work on the project began, in strict secrecy, in the summer of 1974 (not even the firm's chairman, Dennis Poore, was to be told about it). Fortunately the Trident's crankcase was a three-piece design with vertical face joints, and it was a relatively simple exercise to add another centre section while retaining the original end sections. The left-hand section was

Right: *big it certainly is, but the experimental Triumph Quadrant had a compact appearance.*

integral with the gearbox, and in order to preserve the primary and final-drive chain lines, the extra helping of engine would have to hang out to the right – not the best of engineering, of course, but expedient; and cheap.

Standard Trident pistons and connecting rods were to be used, and the four-cylinder block and cylinder head were fashioned by taking two Trident blocks (and heads), cutting off one cylinder from each – the left pot from the right-hand block, and the right pot from the left-hand block, then welding the two pairs of pots together.

One seeming difficulty lay in the crankshaft. As may be recalled, the forged crankshaft of the production three-cylinder model was an ingenious piece of work, initially forged with all three crank throws lying in the same plane; the embryo shaft was then held firmly in the middle while the ends were reheated and twisted to the left and right, so that the cranks became evenly spaced at 120 degrees to each other. But it so happened that one of the experiments Doug had been conducting related to a three-cylinder in which the throws were *not* evenly spaced and, as in the Laverda three, were two-up and one-down. For convenience this experimental crankshaft was a pressed-up item, and so it was simple

to add a further throw, to give the traditional four-cylinder crank arrangement.

Not so easy was manufacture of the camshafts, because had these been made at Kitts Green it would have been all too easy for the 'cat to escape from the bag'. Accordingly, the Quadrant camshafts were produced in a private, very discreet, machine shop. The frame, fuel tank, and cycle parts were BSA Rocket 3 components that had already been used for an experimental (but abandoned) overhead-camshaft three-cylinder, and to minimise the amount by which the engine projected to the right, the unit was moved over to the left just a fraction, the rear-wheel sprocket having to be spaced out from the hub by half an inch to compensate.

There was still the difficulty that the gear pedal, in its normal forward-projecting position, could not operate. The answer was to reverse it, and crank it outward to clear the kick-starter boss, although this did mean that the rider's feet had to be more rearward than was really acceptable. (There was a further answer: transfer the

Presence of the extra crankcase section meant that the gear pedal could not operate normally, and therefore had to be reversed. The folding footrest must be raised before the engine can be kick-started.

Specification

Make Triumph *Model* Quadrant prototype

Capacity 987 cc　　　　　　*Bore and stroke* 67 × 70 mm
Power output Not recorded　*Weight (dry)* Not recorded
Wheelbase 58 in　　　　　　*Price when new* Not marketed
Tyre size: front 4.10 × 19 in; *rear* 4.10 × 19 in

Suspension: front Telescopic, oil-damped
　　　　　　rear Swinging-arm, with spring-and-hydraulic dampers

Manufacturer Norton Triumph International Ltd, Mackadown Lane, Kitts Green, Birmingham

gear change to the left, as was done later on the production Bonneville twins; but at this time all British bikes had right-foot change and there seemed no reason to depart from tradition.)

The Quadrant first took to the road in January 1975, and although no development of any kind was ever carried out on the unit, it proved capable of reaching 119 mph on the MIRA test track. The cams, after all, were only of touring profile, and considering the shoestring-budget pressed-up crankshaft it would have been unwise to try to make the machine go any quicker. The Quadrant was merely a means to an end, a way of seeing as cheaply as possible if an across-the-frame Triumph four was a feasibility.

Sadly, a costing study seemed to show that its manufacture would not be economic (a reflection, really, on the uneconomic methods employed at the one-time BSA plant at Small Heath, where all three-cylinder engines were built on an antiquated, labour-intensive system). Dennis Poore read the study, and stopped all further work on the four, which was

The bank of four carburettors is mounted to the cylinder head by flexible tubing. The twistgroup cable actuates a cross-shaft with four throttle arms.

relegated to a dark corner of the Kitts Green workshop – but not before the author became the first and only journalist to gallop it at rather illegal speeds along Birmingham's Castle Bromwich collector road, parallel to the M6 Motorway. It was beautifully smooth, with plenty of low-down torque and searing acceleration. The gearchange was maybe a little awkward, but with more experience one could have got used to it. And as for the overhang to the right? Totally unnoticeable once the machine was under way.

With the closure of Kitts Green, the Quadrant was smuggled out by Alan Barrett, one of the small team who had worked on the project, but eventually it was returned to NVT to be included in an auction sale of specials, prototypes, and other souvenirs of what had been the great British Motorcycle Industry. Fortunately for future generations, it was bought on behalf of the Museum and rebuilt to the condition in which you see it now.

1960 Velocette 192 cc Model LE

When the Velocette factory announced in October 1948 the coming of the Model LE (the initials simply meant 'Little Engine') the motor cycling public could scarcely have received a bigger shock. After all, Velocette had built their reputation on a range of sturdy traditional singles – the sporty K-model 'cammy Velos', and the solidly worthy high-camshaft overhead-valve M-range: 250 cc MOV, 350 cc MAC, and 500 cc MSS. There had also been a sop to the upper end of the utility market with the two-stroke GTP – which, incidentally, was the first motor cycle of its type to embody throttle-controlled oiling.

But the new LE was something totally out of character. Of only 149 cc (enlargement to 192 cc was to come later), it was a transverse water-cooled flat-twin side-valve, with integral gearbox and shaft final drive, carried in a massive pressed-steel frame member.

The work of designer Charles Udall, it showed evidence of considerable thought. The final-drive shaft, for instance, was housed within the left-hand leg of the cast light-alloy rear pivoted fork, and the upper ends of the rear spring units could be moved through slotted upper mountings in the rear mudguard pressing, to allow for variation in load carried by the machine. Ingenuity was everywhere. Instead of the conventional kick-starter, starting was effected by heaving on a long lever on the right, initial movement of which released then raised the centre stand. For ease of maintenance, the entire subframe comprising engine/gearbox unit and radiator, rear fork and wheel could be detached readily from the main frame member.

Very surprisingly (for it was the Velocette concern which had invented the positive-stop foot change) a hand gearchange lever was featured, operating in a car-type gate. Deeply valanced mudguarding – the front mudguard fixed, the rear a substantial pressing integral with the main beam – inbuilt footboards (two-level, to allow the rider a change of foot position in addition to catering for a pillion rider) and pressed-aluminium legshields all helped to keep the rider dry and warm whatever the weather.

Velocette, in fact, were pursuing that will-o'-the-wisp, the 'motor cycle for the millions'. Anticipating a huge demand for the little twin, they had tooled-up the works at great expense, installing such necessary new plant as heavy presses for producing the frame members. To allow for production space, all existing Velocette models were swept aside.

Right: a two-tone colour scheme, two-level dual seat, and factory-designed pannier boxes indicate a Model LE for the civilian market – but the bulk of LE output was reserved for police urban patrol duty.

Below: the angular lines of the massive pressed-steel frame beam contrast rather strangely with the pressed-steel peardrop-shaped pannier boxes which were offered as official Velocette accessories.

Not a motor cycle for the motor cyclist, the LE was aimed at an untapped market of those who abhorred the 'noisy, smelly, dirty' machines of tradition. Hence water-cooling, adopted in the interests of producing an utterly silent model; in the pursuit of silent running, it was said, even the clicking of the contact-breaker points had been hushed by a spot of careful redesign. That there did indeed exist a non-motor cycling market of those who looked for something new on two wheels was to be proved in years to come, with the arrival of the Vespa and Lambretta scooters from Italy. Sadly, the LE was not the model to tap that market. Maybe it looked too angular. Perhaps the drab grey finish of the first models was a turn-off. Whatever the cause, although the LE did attract a modest following, the orders did not exactly come swarming in.

Velocette persevered (they had to; having expended so much valuable cash on tooling-up, they could not afford to scrap the project now), by first raising the engine capacity to 192 cc, and in later years adopting a four- instead of three-speed gearbox, and a kick-starter instead of the hand-starting lever. In place of all-over grey, a range of two-tone colours became available at option.

They might have done a bit better, had it been

Engine and gearbox, together with the radiator and two-level footboards, could be extracted from the main frame as a sub-assembly for maintenance. Secured by the cylinder-head bolts is an oil filter.

Specification

Make Velocette *Model* LE Water-cooled Mk III

Capacity 192 cc
Power output 10 bhp at 6,000 rpm
Bore and stroke 50 × 49 mm
Weight (dry) 250 lb
Price when new £196 0s 4d
Wheelbase 51.25 in
Tyre size: front 3.25 × 18 in; *rear* 3.25 × 18 in

Suspension: front Telescopic, undamped
          rear Swinging-arm, with spring-and-hydraulic dampers

Manufacturer Veloce Ltd, York Road, Hall Green, Birmingham 28

possible to bring the engine up to full 250 cc capacity, but having been laid out initially as a one-fifty, the crankshaft was not really man enough to handle any big increase in power. However, if the public at large was to spurn the Model LE (and to keep the factory occupied, Velocettes had been forced to bring back the overhead-valve singles), the machine was at last to find acceptance in one particular field. The police had been looking for a quiet-running urban beat patrol machine, and they found exactly the thing in the LE. Several

Below: *the drive shaft to the rear wheel assembly is housed within the left-side arm of the cast-light-alloy pivoted rear fork.*

thousands were taken into service by the Metropolitan Police, Birmingham City Police, and many other large towns – and the manufacturers found that the story about the size of a copper's feet had substance, because they had to fit police-model LEs with reinforced brake pedals!

And so the LE became the police 'Noddy Bike', a name which had nothing to do with the hero of Enid Blyton's nursery tales. It arose from a directive issued to LE-riding Metropolitan Police constables. A foot-patrol policeman, on meeting his sergeant or a senior officer, was required to salute. This, however, could not be done while riding – at least, not without raising one hand from the handlebars and risking a wobble. To

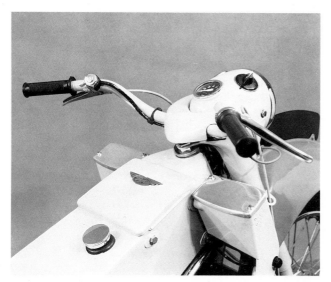

preserve the tradition, therefore, the motor cyclist would show respect to the sergeant by affording him a smart inclination of the head. In other words, a definite nod.

Some, but by no means all, police LEs were fitted with high-output generators to power radio sets (and with enlarged compartments in the top of the frame beam, to house the necessary batteries) but specifications could be varied according to the needs of the constabulary concerned. The LE was to remain in production to the very end of Velocette in 1971 (an LE was the second-last machine to come off the assembly line) but by then its police career was almost over, its work having been taken over by the new Panda cars. There were plenty of policemen who considered the change to cars to be a retrograde step. The 'Noddy Bike' copper may have been motorised, but he was visible and human, which the beat man enclosed in a tin-box Panda car was not.

1967 Velocette 499 cc Thruxton

Both the Triumph and Velocette companies at one time had a model known as the Thruxton in their respective catalogues, for the same very logical reason. Thruxton is the name of an airfield near Andover, Hampshire, where in the 1950s and 1960s the Southampton Club organised a production-machine marathon race around the perimeter track. Originally this event was known as the Thruxton Nine-Hour; later mileage rather than time became the controlling factor and the name was changed to the Thruxton 500-Mile.

Regulations ensured that the competing machines should be as sold to the public (although certain modifications were permitted in the interests of safety). Naturally, no rider could be expected to stay in the saddle non-stop for nine hours or 500 miles as the case may be, and so each competing machine was shared by two riders taking turn about, the change-over usually coinciding with the need for refuelling.

It was a type of sport that suited the big-single Velocette admirably, and prominence of the 499 cc Venom in early Thruxton events led to the introduction from 1964 of a high-performance kit comprising a new cylinder head with downdraught inlet track and Amal Grand Prix carburettor, narrowed valve angle and bigger inlet valve. In turn, room had to be found for the bigger and more steeply-angled carburettor, and that meant fitting a new fuel tank with the rear right-hand corner cut away, and an oil tank with a scoop in the top face.

The kit was understandably expensive, but if a man was to take production racing seriously expense was a relatively minor consideration. In any case, it was a temporary measure, because from 1965 a true super-sports Venom entered the catalogue. This was the Thruxton, named in acknowledgement of previous Velocette achievements at that venue, and not only did it incorporate the full racing kit as detailed earlier, but there was a seat with raised back so that the rider could really get flat down to it, and rear-set footrests and control pedals so that he was in total command while in a racing crouch. Up front, for the first time, was a powerful twin-leading-shoe brake made by John Tickle.

It was ironic that in the very year the Velocette Thruxton made its bow, the organising Southampton Club should break away from the Thruxton track and, instead, stage the 1965 500-Mile on a very different airfield circuit, at Castle Combe, Wiltshire. All the same, the 500 cc class was still dominated by Velocettes, with the Howard German/Chris Williams

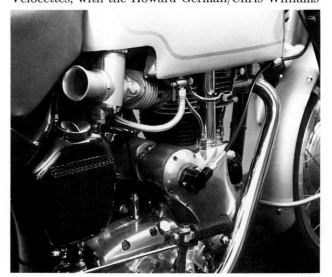

Taking its name from the famous long-distance production-machine race in which it was especially successful, the Velocette Thruxton was in essence a tuned version of the 499 cc Venom.

To accommodate the downdraught Amal TT10 carburettor, the rear corner of the Velocette Thruxton's fuel tank had to be cut away. The finned carburettor mounting stub was almost a Thruxton trademark.

model taking the initial lead until put out by a broken connecting rod. Then the Velocette of Ellis Boyce/Tom Phillips took over as class leader until the machine was retired at half distance with lost compression. There were still more Velocettes just waiting for a chance, and in the end it was the Thruxton shared by Joe Dunphy and David Dixon, fast making up time lost through a stop to dry-out a water-logged magneto, which gained the chequered flag.

It was always the contention of traditional British motor cycle makers (and none was more traditional than Velocette, a firm founded by, and run throughout its life by, the Goodman family) that racing improved the breed. Lessons learned from production racing were passed through to the standard models, and so the Thruxton-type front fork and twin-leading-shoe front brake became standard practice for the 350 cc Viper and 500 cc Venom roadsters also.

The model chosen for the National Motorcycle Museum collection dates from 1967, in which year the 500-Mile production race marathon found yet another home, this time Brands Hatch circuit in Kent. For a time it seemed that there would be the inevitable Velocette victory in the 500 cc class, for with just one hour to go the Reg Everett/Tom Phillips Thruxton was

Three holes in the side plate of the full-width rear hub give access to the studs securing the hub to the brake drum assembly. The Smith's worm-drive gearbox for the speedometer cable is carried on the rear spindle.

eight laps clear of the nearest rival. But then the magneto ceased to spark, the machine stopped, and all that could be done was wait just clear of the finish line until the flag went out, then push across to claim fourth place.

However, Velocette honour was retrieved in the Isle of Man. There in 1967 the Auto Cycle Union promoted the first-ever Production Machine TT, and Neil Kelly and Keith Heckles made it a Velocette Thruxton benefit by finishing first and second in the 500 cc section. Kelly's race average was 89.89 mph, astonishing for what was really a hotted-up roadster.

Indeed, for all its racing prowess, the Velocette Thruxton remained a useful long-distance road model for the hard rider, and with full lighting equipment and the traditional lozenge silencer with perforated fishtail, it was still thoroughly tractable in city traffic – or even in deep snow, where one Thruxton-owning Dragon Rally enthusiast found it would chug along without protest at 15 to 20 mph in bottom gear. That,

Right: to allow the strength of the rear springing to be adjusted to suit varying passenger loads, the upper mounting bolts of the rear damper unit can be moved through an arc, a suitable slotted track being provided.

Specification

Make Velocette *Model* Thruxton

Capacity 499 cc
Power output 41 bhp at
    6,200 rpm
Wheelbase 53.75 in
Tyre size: front 3.00 × 19 in; *rear* 3.25 × 19 in

Bore and stroke 86 × 86 mm
Weight (dry) 375 lb
Price when new £385 13s 6d

Suspension: front Telescopic, oil-damped
           rear Swinging-arm, with spring-and-hydraulic dampers

Manufacturer Veloce Ltd, York Road, Hall Green, Birmingham 28

though, was with the machine in 1969 specification, by which time Velocettes had had to give up the traditional magneto (because Lucas no longer made one) and, instead, adopt coil ignition. Privately, there were those who felt that the firm should have fitted coil ignition long ago, for not only did it improve flexibility but it got over the old Velocette bugbear of difficult kick-starting.

To a present-day rider, the Velocette handlebar control arrangement resembles a Christmas tree, but each lever has a purpose. On the left bar is the clutch lever, valve-lifter trigger (for ease of starting) and manual ignition advance. On the right is the brake lever, carburettor choke control and dipswitch.

Road-tested by *Motor Cycle*, the Thruxton returned a highest one-way speed of 114 mph, although that was with the assistance of a tail wind, admittedly, and the two-way mean was 104 mph. What might really astonish riders of modern machinery was that a production-race machine should have a fuel consumption figure at a steady 30 mph of 96 mpg! Even at 70 mph, the fall was to no more than 58 mpg, Amal Grand Prix carburettor and 2 in-diameter inlet valve notwithstanding! Power output was 41 bhp at 6,200 rpm.

The Thruxton represented the ultimate stage in the development of the high-camshaft, short-pushrod M-series Velocettes that had begun back in 1934, and performance had been pushed so high as to be on a par with what had once been regarded as the superlative racing machine, the 350 cc overhead-camshaft Velocette Mk VIII. It was a pretty remarkable achievement.

1951 Vincent 499 cc Series C Grey Flash

From its very earliest days the Vincent, and its forerunner the HRD, always did have a close association with road-racing. Indeed, Howard R. Davies – the man who founded the marque in the mid-1920s – made TT history by winning the 1921 Senior TT on a 350 cc AJS. It was only natural that Davies, on starting a factory of his own, should want to cash-in on his personal racing glory by supporting a racing policy, and both he and Yorkshire's wild man Freddie Dixon were to bring the name HRD to the forefront.

Later, after Phil Vincent had acquired the HRD goodwill and, by adding his own name, formed the Vincent-HRD Company, he would continue to seek publicity through road-racing, using Rudge and JAP engines at first. However, it was the failure of proprietary power units in the Vincent-HRD's works TT models of 1934 that led to the 'Great Decision'. Never again, declared Phil Vincent, would the firm pin its faith in engines produced by outside factories. From now on, the Vincent-HRD would be powered by an engine of the firm's own design and manufacture.

And so the first 499 cc ohv Comet – designed by Phil Irving, and eventually to be known as the Series A – came into being. You may have heard, too, the legend that one day Phil Irving just happened to place two tracings of the Comet engine on top of each other but at an angle; and that gave him the inspiration for the 998 cc vee-twin Rapide.

When the Vincent-HRD returned to production at the end of the Second World War, the first priority was to satisfy the overseas demand for the big vee-twin roadsters (in tidied-up form, as the Series B). But racing was part of the Vincent-HRD heritage, and it was inevitable that the firm would return to the road-race scene as soon as was practical.

The vehicle for this re-entry was the 499 cc Series C Grey Flash, introduced in 1949 and basically a tuned version of the Comet roadster. The tuning was mainly

Vincent's track-racing 500 cc Grey Flash single was the model on which young John Surtees, an apprentice at the factory, had his first taste of fame.

In essence the Grey Flash was the front half of a Vincent vee-twin, a factor which certainly helped with spares, but it was to earn a track reputation in its own right.

undertaken by the brothers George and Cliff Brown, and the outcome was a five-hundred which, in stripped form, was capable of a most respectable 115 mph. Power output was 35 bhp at 6,200 rpm.

To a very large extent, the Grey Flash could be considered as a single-cylinder version of the 998 cc Black Lightning racer, being tuned to the same specification. As originally presented, it was equipped with a Burman gearbox, but as development proceeded this was replaced by a racing Albion. Brake plates were in Elektron magnesium alloy, the carburettor was a TT Amal, and weight-paring brought the machine to a race-ready 330 lb.

In fact, three variants of the Grey Flash were shown in the catalogue, with the stripped racer at £275 plus purchase tax, a super-sports-roadster at £290 plus pt, and the super-sports-roadster convertible to racing trim at £300 plus pt. To show faith in their own product, Vincent entered a full team in the 1950 Senior TT, comprising Ken Bills, Manliff Barrington, and C. A. Stevens. The works entries were trying-out an experimental type of big-end bearing, but this was disastrous and only Ken Bills was to be classed as a

finisher, in 12th place at 83.79 mph. Nor did works entries in the 1951 Senior TT meet with any better success, but fortunately for Vincent-HRD honour a young apprentice at the factory was beginning to make quite a name for himself, racing a Grey Flash on the mainland short circuits. He was John Surtees, and,

Liberal drilling of the footrest mounting plate was adopted in the interests of saving weight. Drilling in the rear of the primary chaincase, however, helped cool the clutch.

Specification

Make Vincent HRD *Model* Grey Flash

Capacity 499 cc	*Bore and stroke* 84 × 90 mm
Power output 35 bhp at	*Weight (dry)* 330 lb
6,200 rpm	*Price when new* £381 0s 0d
Wheelbase 55.75 in	

Tyre size: front 3.00 × 21 in; *rear* 3.50 × 20 in

Suspension: front 'Girdraulic', oil-damped
  rear Cantilever, with twin spring boxes and hydraulic dampers

Manufacturer The Vincent-HRD Co Ltd, Great North Road, Stevenage, Hertfordshire

In the cantilever suspension system, undamped springs are housed in the outer two telescopic housings, while a hydraulic damper is mounted in the middle.

together with another privateer named John Hodgkin, made sure that there was usually a Grey Flash somewhere in the awards list.

Commercially, however, the Grey Flash was not really a success, and it remained on offer between 1949 and 1951 only. The example displayed here is from the final production run and represents the Grey Flash in its ultimate stage of development, dressed overall in the grey-green livery which gave the model its name.

Essentially, the engine is the front half of a Vincent vee-twin, suspended by the cylinder head in characteristic fashion from a spine frame beam which serves also as the oil tank. Suspension is unique, for no production Vincent was ever fitted with a telescopic front fork, and here we have the famous Series C Vincent Girdraulic fork – basically a girder pattern, but with the sophistication of long hydraulic struts mounted at the rear of each fork blade. Cantilever suspension is featured at the rear, the entire rear sub-frame pivoting under the control of twin spring boxes mounted

George Brown's name is usually associated with those magnificent record-breaking Vincent twins, Nero and Super Nero. But he was a TT competitor too, though in practice for the 1950 Senior race he had to withdraw through illness. His Grey Flash, seen here, was then taken over by Ken Bills, who went on to finish twelfth.

beneath the seat; a small telescopic damper is carried between the spring boxes.

One final observation. When he first started in business, Phil Vincent had gone to considerable trouble to purchase the HRD trademark from its previous owner, and there might be some puzzlement among readers as to why, from 1950, he should have dropped the famous initials from the now well-known Vincent-HRD programme. The bikes from that point on were known as just plain Vincent (although, because stocks of existing castings had to be used up, the old name could still be seen on certain parts of the machine for some while to come).

The answer lies on the far side of the Atlantic, where the native big vee-twin was the Harley-Davidson, known colloquially as the 'HD'. It was Phil Vincent's American dealer network which persuaded him to drop HRD; it seems, motor cyclists in the USA had some sort of crazy idea that the Vincent was a kind of Limey relation of the Harley. How wrong could anyone get!

Left: twin single-leading-shoe front brake drums afforded excellent stopping power by contemporary standards. The front fork is the famed 'Girdraulic', the parallel-ruler blade action being controlled by long and slim hydraulic struts on the rear of each leg.

1956 Vincent 998 cc Series D Black Prince

The hand-built products of Phil Vincent's little factory at Stevenage, on the Great North Road, always were just that bit special. They appealed particularly to a discerning few – and therein lay the seeds of the marque's own destruction, perhaps. Vincent tried various expediencies to bring more money into the business: the Amanda water scooter, a good idea which foundered because the technology of glass-fibre hull construction was as yet imperfectly understood; a link-up with NSU, whereby Vincent would assemble NSU lightweights in England and add a proportion of local content, failed to get very far off the ground; and nobody was going to get very fat by marketing a 50 cc cycle auxiliary motor, no matter how good the Vincent Firefly may have been.

By the mid-1950s overall sales of motor cycles in Britain were nose-diving. This was for a number of reasons but mainly because of an increase in affluence; with more money to spend those who might in earlier times have opted for a motor cycle could now afford a small car. Conversely, the age of the status symbol – when the self-made man would park a high-powered motor cycle alongside his Bentley in the garage, for use only on warm and sunny days – had yet to dawn. And that was a shade unfortunate for Phil Vincent, whose illustrious vee-twins especially were status symbols awaiting the dawn.

Something had to be done, he felt, to stimulate sales. There was little point in giving the big Vincents added performance, for they already produced as much

Beneath the extensive glass-fibre bodywork was a simplified frame and rear suspension, but the engine was the familiar high-camshaft vee-twin.

performance as a road rider could reasonably be expected to handle. And so Vincent opted to go in an entirely new direction, by clothing his existing machines in an all-enveloping glass-fibre casing, incorporating legshields, handlebar fairing and hand muffs, and a perspex windscreen. In his view, such a machine could be ridden to the office by executive types, without the need to dress up in bulky anti-weather clothing. It was the same thinking that had influenced the designers of such lesser machines as the

Total enclosure by glass-fibre panelling was a surprise departure for a factory which had previously gloried in the exposed nature of its power units. The 998 cc Series D Black Prince was the flagship of the Vincent range.

Ariel Leader and LE Velocette – only more so, for here was weather protection allied to exhilarating performance.

Nor was it just the enclosure, startling though that undoubtedly was. So that the city gent could park his enclosed Vincent on arrival with the minimum of effort, Phil revived the old pre-war Rudge idea of a centre stand operated from the saddle by pulling a long hand lever on the left of the machine. Construction of the 'frame' (such as it was) was completely new. In place of the former fabricated upper member which incorporated the oil tank, there was now a single tubular strut bolted at the front end to the forged steering-head assembly; at the rear the forward mounting of the new single spring/damper unit now replaced the old twin-spring-box Vincent arrangement.

As displayed at the 1954 Earls Court Show there were three all-enclosed Vincents for the new season – the 500 cc Victor, and 998 cc Black Knight and Black Prince twins, replacing respectively the familiar Comet single, and Rapide and Black Shadow twins. As it happens, however, the Victor never did go into production, and one prototype only was built. The machine featured here is the top model of the trio, the Series D Black Prince, which employed the formidable Black Shadow power unit.

At Earls Court, the unusual appearance of the new Vincents attracted comment in plenty, much of it unfavourable – the British motor cyclist is conservative by nature and he thought it sacrilege to hide the beautiful machinery of a Vincent big twin behind an anonymous sheet of plastic. No doubt there was some technical reason for the forward-facing 'beaks' at the top of each built-in legshield, but they were heartily disliked by the public, nonetheless.

Moreover, Phil Vincent had the misfortune to sub-contract manufacture of the glass-fibre mouldings to an outside contractor whose products fell a little short of the quality he sought, and pending the awarding of a new contract to another supplier he was forced to produce an unclothed Series D range for a while, simply to keep the workforce occupied.

Even so, events were fast overtaking the Vincent works, and Phil Vincent at last had to face the fact that

Specification

Make Vincent *Model* Series D Black Prince

Capacity 998 cc	*Bore and stroke* 84 × 90 mm
Power output 55 bhp at 5,750 rpm	*Weight (dry)* 460 lb
Wheelbase 56.5 in	*Price when new* £378 0s 0d

Tyre size: front 4.50 × 19 in; *rear* 4.00 × 18 in

Suspension: front 'Girdraulic', oil-damped
　　　　　rear Cantilever monoshock, oil-damped

Manufacturer Vincent Engineers Ltd, Great North Road, Stevenage, Hertfordshire

Left: *an enclosed Series D version of the top-of-the-range Black Shadow, the Black Prince represented the final development stage of the Vincent before the factory closed.*

Right: *the forward peaks to the side enclosure panels were designed to channel cooling air to the engine. Styling of the high-mounted headlamp cowl and short handshields is uncomfortable. Note the hand-lever-operated centre stand, an echo of pre-war Rudge practice.*

motor cycle production – especially of a low-volume product aimed at the very top end of the market – was an unprofitable exercise. Financial investigation was to show that the firm was losing money on each bike they sold. Reluctantly, the decision was taken to close down the motor cycle side of the business (although, in fact, production of industrial engines was to continue for some time yet). In all, only 460 Vincents were built in the whole of 1955, and only 200 of those were of the enclosed type.

The very last Vincent to leave the assembly line was a 998 cc Black Prince, on December 16th, 1955, although a handful more were to be built up subsequently from spares. Naturally, it would take a few weeks for the final batch to reach the customers and become registered for the road so these, technically, were 1956 models; among that very last batch was the machine now in the National Motorcycle Musuem collection.

The widely-spaced pushrod tubes are typical of Stevenage practice. The long scythe-like kick-starter shank was expedient, but hardly handsome!

Studying the machine as now exhibited, a visitor might well wonder how a motor cycle so voluminously covered might handle in a side wind, or if the enclosure would muffle or enhance the Vincent's throaty bark. And what would be the effect on fuel consumption? Luckily for us, *The Motor Cycle* did manage to road-test an enclosed twin (albeit a Black Knight) before the end, concluding that it handled as precisely as any other Vincent, noise level was lower, and the air-smoothing bodywork actually improved the consumption.

The Black Prince never was put through the timing lights to ascertain maximum performance. For that matter, neither was the Black Shadow, which the same magazine tested in 1949, but 110 mph was recorded in *third* gear, and though a flash reading of 118 mph was attained in top, the tester commented that at that the bike was still accelerating and had yet to reach maximum! After all, a 55 bhp output at 5,700 rpm can push a motor cycle along like nobody's business!

The National Motorcycle Museum

The twenty five motorcycles profiled in this book are just a small part of the National Motorcycle Museum's display of almost 500 machines.

Over the eighty-odd years since the first motorcycle wobbled down our roads, over five hundred different makers have placed machines on the market – some succeeded, some did not. There are examples of both in the museum.

That is the key to the Museum – it is dedicated to preserving motorcycles made in Britain, successful or not. No other motorcycle museum is on the same scale, and none are devoted to the machines of just one country's industry. For that reason it is a unique undertaking.

The National Motorcycle Museum is a living entity and it is still growing. And it needs help to continue to build. As a registered charity the Museum depends upon donations from the public and its own fund-raising activities to develop and maintain its place as the World's foremost museum of British Motorcycles.

Two of the Museum's major fund raising activities are designed to give individuals a stake in the Museum's future.

Friends Of The Museum

People who elect to become a 'Friend Of The Museum' join a group of other enthusiasts who are interested in the success of the National Motorcycle Museum, and wish to help on an on-going basis. To become a 'Friend Of The Museum' costs a very reasonable £5 per year, or £75 for Life Membership.

Yard Of Land

In addition it is possible to help the Museum by buying a 'Yard Of Land' or more for £10. Each plot of land has a separate 'title' and will be marked on a special grid in the Museum, with the donor's name recorded in a special book, which will be exhibited in the Museum.

If you would like to become a 'Friend Of The Museum' or buy a 'Yard Of Land', or both, please write to W. R. Richards, 86 Henwood Lane, Catherine-de-Barnes, Solihull, West Midlands, B91 2TH.

1917 1,000 cc twin cylinder Royal Ruby, before and after restoration